INTERPRETATIONS OF LIFE
AND MIND

INTERPRETATIONS OF LIFE AND MIND

Essays around the Problem of Reduction

Edited by
MARJORIE GRENE

Contributors

Ilya Prigogine
Charles Taylor
Anthony J. P. Kenny
Amélie Rorty
Alasdair C. MacIntyre
Hubert Dreyfus
William T. Scott
Robert S. Cohen

NEW YORK: HUMANITIES PRESS

First published in The United States of America 1971
by Humanities Press Incorporated
303 Park Avenue South
New York, N.Y. 10010
Printed in Great Britain
© Routledge & Kegan Paul Ltd 1971

Library of Congress Catalog Card No. 76–150237

ISBN 0–391–00144–2

Presented by the Study Group
to
MICHAEL POLANYI
for
his eightieth birthday
11 March 1971

Schiksaalsgesez ist diss, dass Alle sich erfahren,
Dass, wenn die Stille kehrt, auch eine Sprache sei.

CONTENTS

Acknowledgments   viii

Preface   ix

Meetings of the Study Group on the Unity of
Knowledge October 1967–March 1970   xi

1 Unity of Physical Laws and
   Levels of Description   Ilya Prigogine   1

2 Reducibility: Another Side
   Issue?   Marjorie Grene   14

3 How is Mechanism
   Conceivable?   Charles Taylor   38

4 The Homunculus Fallacy   Anthony J. P. Kenny   65
   Not Every Homunculus
   Spoils the Argument   Amélie Rorty   75
   Reply to Mrs Rorty   Anthony J. P. Kenny   81

5 Behavior, Belief and Emotion Alasdair C. MacIntyre   84

6 The Critique of Artificial
   Reason   Hubert Dreyfus   99

7 Tacit Knowledge and the
   Concept of Mind   William T. Scott   117

8 Tacit, Social and Hopeful   Robert S. Cohen   137

   Bibliography   149

   Index   151

ACKNOWLEDGMENTS

The meetings of the Study Group, as well as the preparation and publication of this volume, were made possible by a grant from the Ford Foundation to the University of California at Davis.

There are other debts of gratitude which we also wish to acknowledge here. Thanks are due to our hosts on various occasions: the University of Montreal, M.I.T., the University of Texas at Austin, the Rockefeller Foundation and the staff of the Villa Serbelloni, Boston University and Rockefeller University; to our indefatigable executive secretary, Mr George Gale, who steered us through an endless maze of travel arrangements, with the help of Mrs Mary Pressley of the U.C.D. accounting office; to our editorial assistant, Mrs Diana T. Hewitt, and the Study Group office staff, including at various times Mrs Tosca Arbini, Miss Christine Bender, Miss Anna Pechanec, and Miss Judy Williams.

PREFACE

'By convention hot, by convention cold,' said Democritus, 'by convention sweet, by convention bitter; only the atoms and the void are real.' And so too then, it seems, for 'good and bad', even, in the heel of the hunt, for 'true and false'.

That 'only' of Democritus still haunts us. Yet a harmless haunting, one may say; or even beneficial, if, as many believe, scientific explanation—which, above all else, has made our world—is essentially reductive and particulate.

Such crude reductivism is still widespread and its influence wide-ranging: from scientists' and social scientists' reflections on their own methods to formulations of the nature of language, the role of art, the foundations and reach of human values.

The aim of the Study Group has been to combat this dogmatism by examining its premises and implications, and by working, in a number of diverse but interrelated areas, toward the construction of a viable alternative. Such an alternative can be achieved, we believe, not by attempting to exempt life or mind or culture from the operation of the universal laws of nature (a move of which persistent reductivists still accuse us),* but by producing, on new premises, a more adequate comprehensive view of science, of nature and of man.

Ars longa, vita brevis; and when the art in question is that of remaking our basic perspective on the world, the task is both long and sometimes devious. However confidently we share our common goals, we must work each with his own tools at his own pace in the hope of building severally yet jointly a stable and harmonious edifice.

A number of our meetings have been concerned, directly or

* E.g., Professor Hilary Putnam at our 1969 Berkeley conference: all anti-reductivists, he asserted, are 'exceptionalists'.

ix

indirectly, with the problem of reducibility or reduction: of biology to physics, of mind to the central nervous system, of the person and his expressions to behavior, of minds to machines, of heuristic imagination to the bare bones of a formal system. The papers collected here partly spring from, partly bear on, these discussions.

MEETINGS OF THE STUDY GROUP ON THE UNITY OF KNOWLEDGE OCTOBER 1967–MARCH 1970

'*Artificial Intelligence*', *Massachusetts Institute of Technology, 6–7 October 1967*

Participants:
Professor Paul Benacerraf, Princeton University
Professor J. Bronowski, Salk Institute for Biological Studies
Professor Noam Chomsky, Massachusetts Institute of Technology
Professor Hubert Dreyfus, Massachusetts Institute of Technology
Professor Kenneth Forster, Massachusetts Institute of Technology
Professor Lon L. Fuller, Harvard University
Professor Marjorie Grene, University of California, Davis
Mr John R. Lucas, Merton College, Oxford
Professor Edward Pols, Bowdoin College
Professor Hilary Putnam, Harvard University
Dr M. Ross Quillian, Balt, Beranek and Newman, Cambridge, Massachusetts
Professor Abner Shimony, Massachusetts Institute of Technology
Professor John R. Silber, University of Texas, Austin
Professor Charles Taylor, McGill University and University of Montreal

'*Value Freedom*', *University of Montreal, 23–25 February 1968*

Participants:
Professor Hubert Dreyfus, Massachusetts Institute of Technology

Professor Heinz Eulau, Stanford University
Professor Marjorie Grene, University of California, Davis
Professor Sigmund Koch, University of Texas, Austin
Professor Alasdair MacIntyre, University of Essex
Mr Alan Montefiore, Merton College, Oxford
Professor Edward Pols, Bowdoin College
Professor John R. Silber, University of Texas, Austin
Professor Charles Taylor, McGill University and University of
    Montreal
Professor Walter A. Weisskopf, Roosevelt University

*'The (Ir)reducibility of Biology to Physics and Chemistry',
University of Texas, Austin, 20–21 April 1968*

Participants:
Professor Francisco Ayala, Rockefeller University
Professor H. J. Barr, University of Wisconsin
Professor Robert Causey, University of Texas, Austin
Professor Hubert Dreyfus, Massachusetts Institute of Tech-
    nology
Professor Marjorie Grene, University of California, Davis
Dr W. Roy Jackson, Queen's University, Belfast
Professor Alasdair MacIntyre, University of Essex
Professor Michael Menaker, University of Texas, Austin
Professor Robert Palter, University of Texas, Austin
Professor Michael Polanyi, Oxford
Professor Ilya Prigogine, Free University of Brussels
Professor Richard H. Richardson, University of Texas, Austin
Professor Charles Taylor, McGill University and University of
    Montreal
Professor Michael S. Watanabe, University of Hawaii
Professor Richard Zaner, University of Texas, Austin

*'The Programmability of Piaget', University of Montreal,
30 May 1968*

Participants:
Professor Hubert Dreyfus, Massachusetts Institute of Tech-
    nology
Professor Niko Frijda, Psychologisch Laboratorium, Amster-
    dam

Professor Jean-Blaise Grize, University of Neuchatel, Switzerland

Professor Alasdair MacIntyre, University of Essex

Professor Seymour Papert, Massachusetts Institute of Technology

Professor Jean Piaget, University of Geneva

Professor Charles Taylor, McGill University and University of Montreal

Professor Gilbert Voyat, Massachusetts Institute of Technology

'*Art and Perception*', *Villa Serbelloni, Bellagio, Italy, 28 July– 3 August 1968*

Participants:
Professor Rudolf Arnheim, Harvard University
Mr Michael Ayrton, Toppesfield near Halstead, Essex, England
Mr J. O. Bayley, New College, Oxford
Professor Ernest H. Gombrich, Warburg Institute
Professor Richard Gregory, University of Edinburgh
Professor Marjorie Grene, University of California, Davis
Miss Iris Murdoch, Steeple Aston, Oxon, England
Professor Michael Polanyi, Oxford
Professor Edward Pols, Bowdoin College
Professor Joseph Rykwert, University of Essex
Professor Otto von Simson, Free University of Berlin
Mr Michael Tanner, Corpus Christi College, Cambridge

'*The Logic of Conversation*', *University of California, Davis, 30 November–1 December 1968*

Participants:
Professor Ronald Arbini, University of California, Davis
Professor Gordon Bermant, University of California, Davis
Professor Bennet Berger, University of California, Davis
Professor Hubert Dreyfus, University of California, Berkeley
Professor Harold Garfinkel, University of California, Los Angeles
Professor H. Paul Grice, University of California, Berkeley
Professor Marjorie Grene, University of California, Davis
Professor Sigmund Koch, University of Texas, Austin

Professor Alasdair MacIntyre, University of Essex
Professor John Malcolm, University of California, Davis
Professor Lloyd Reinhardt, University of California, Santa
    Barbara
Professor Dorothy E. Smith, University of British Columbia
Professor Barry Stroud, University of California, Berkeley
Professor Charles Taylor, McGill University and University of
    Montreal
Professor Samuel Todes, Northwestern University
Professor Donald Weismann, University of Texas, Austin

'*Scientific Knowledge and Discovery*', University of Texas,
Austin, 29–30 March 1969

Participants:
Professor Robert S. Cohen, Boston University
Professor Marjorie Grene, University of California, Davis
Professor Keith Gunderson, University of Minnesota
Dr Rom Harré, Linacre College, Oxford
Professor Sigmund Koch, University of Texas, Austin
Professor Paul Lorenzen, University of Erlangen and University
    of Texas, Austin
Professor Alasdair MacIntyre, University of Essex
Professor Michael Polanyi, Oxford
Professor Ilya Prigogine, Free University of Brussels
Professor William Scott, University of Nevada
Professor John R. Silber, University of Texas, Austin
Professor Charles Taylor, McGill University and University of
    Montreal
Professor Marx Wartofsky, Boston University
Professor Donald Weismann, University of Texas, Austin

'*Concepts of Mind*', University of California, Berkeley,
23–28 August 1969

Participants:
Professor William Arrowsmith, University of Texas, Austin
Professor Ronald Arbini, University of California, Davis
Professor Jarvis Bastian, University of California, Davis

Professor Gordon Bermant, University of California, Davis
Professor Thomas Bever, Rockefeller University
Professor Hubert Dreyfus, University of California, Berkeley
Dr Frank Ervin, Harvard University
Professor Norman Geschwind, Harvard University
Professor J. J. Gibson, Cornell University
Professor Richard Gregory, University of Edinburgh
Professor Marjorie Grene, University of California, Davis
Professor Alan Grinnell, University of California, Los Angeles
Professor Keith Gunderson, University of Minnesota
Dr Anthony J. Kenny, Balliol College, Oxford
Professor Leszek Kolakowski, University of California, Berkeley
Professor Jonas Langer, University of California, Berkeley
Professor John McCarthy, Stanford University
Professor Alasdair MacIntyre, University of Essex
Professor Alan Newell, Carnegie-Mellon University
Professor Karl H. Pribram, Stanford University
Professor Hilary Putnam, Harvard University
Professor Amélie Rorty, Rutgers State University
Professor Richard Rorty, Princeton University
Professor Arthur L. Samuel, Stanford University
Professor Michael Scriven, University of California, Berkeley
Professor John Searle, University of California, Berkeley
Professor John R. Silber, University of Texas, Austin
Professor Richard W. Sperry, California Institute of Technology
Professor Barry Stroud, University of California, Berkeley
Professor Charles Taylor, McGill University and University of Montreal
Professor Samuel J. Todes, Northwestern University
Professor Hao Wang, Rockefeller University
Dr Joseph Weizenbaum, Massachusetts Institute of Technology
Professor Oliver L. Zangwill, Psychological Laboratory, Cambridge

'Scientific Discovery', Boston University, 18–19 October 1969

Participants:
Professor Joseph Agassi, Boston University
Professor Sylvain Bromberger, Massachusetts Institute of Technology

Professor Robert S. Cohen, Boston University
Professor Hubert Dreyfus, University of California, Berkeley
Professor Marjorie Grene, University of California, Davis
Dr Rom Harré, Linacre College, Oxford
Professor Alasdair MacIntyre, University of Essex
Dr Jagdish Mehra, University of Texas, Austin
Professor Leonard K. Nash, Harvard University
Professor Abner Shimony, Boston University
Professor E. C. George Sudarshan, University of Texas, Austin
Professor Charles Taylor, McGill University and University of Montreal
Professor Marx W. Wartofsky, Boston University

'*Psychological Models*', *Rockefeller University, 28–29 March 1970*

Participants:
Professor Thomas Bever, Rockefeller University
Dr Susan Cary, Harvard University
Professor Robert S. Cohen, Boston University
Professor Hubert Dreyfus, University of California, Berkeley
Professor Jerry Fodor, Massachusetts Institute of Technology
Professor Marjorie Grene, University of California, Davis
Dr A. R. Jonckheere, University College, London
Professor Alasdair MacIntyre, University of Essex
Professor Karl H. Pribram, Stanford University
Professor Norman S. Sutherland, University of Sussex
Professor Charles Taylor, McGill University and University of Montreal
Professor Hao Wang, Rockefeller University
Professor Marx W. Wartofsky, Boston University

1

UNITY OF PHYSICAL LAWS AND LEVELS OF DESCRIPTION

Ilya Prigogine

In the view of the reductivists, all science, and biology in particular, is reducible to physics; all the laws of science can be systematically connected with and derived from the fundamental laws of matter in motion. The minimal step in rebutting this position is to demonstrate that physics itself can generate methods for describing, not only classical systems, tending toward maximum entropy, but *structures*, configurations which exhibit growth at least, perhaps eventually self-maintenance and self-replication. Professor Prigogine, along with an increasing number of biophysicists and biochemists, such as Eigen and Katchalsky, is the chief proponent of this view.

I INTRODUCTION

It is a very interesting coincidence that the idea of evolution emerges in the science of the nineteenth century in two conflicting ways:

(a) In thermodynamics the second law is formulated. As is well known, according to this law the entropy increases in a *closed* system. This increase describes essentially the tendency of the system to reach a state of maximum disorder. Since Boltzmann we know that entropy is a measure of 'disorder', of 'randomness'. Therefore the second law of thermodynamics is the law of progressive disorganization, of destruction of existing structures. Since its formulation, this law has appeared to most physicists as one of the greatest achievements of theoretical physics, as one of the corner stones of our understanding of the physical world.

(b) On the contrary, in biology or in sociology the idea of evolution is closely associated with an increase of organization with the creation of more and more complex structures.

1

It is clear that both concepts have deep philosophical implications. The extension of the thermodynamical concept of evolution to the world as a whole leads to the idea that 'structure' existed mainly in some far distant past, in a kind of 'golden age'. Since then, the world has been dissolving in a progressive chaos. The biological concept of evolution points precisely toward the opposite direction. Nobody has better expressed it than Bergson, whose whole metaphysics is essentially a meditation on the biology of his time: 'The deeper we go into the nature of time, the more we understand that duration means invention, creation of forms, continuous elaboration of what is absolutely new.'[1] To some extent the ideas of Spencer are similar. He indeed believes that the basic principle of the evolution of nature is the principle of the 'instability of the homogeneous'.[2]

How can one reconcile these two aspects of evolution? There is no doubt that both correspond to different aspects of physical reality. If we consider two liquids and permit them to mix, diffusion takes place. This progressive forgetting of initial conditions is a typical example of situations described by an increase of entropy. On the contrary in biological systems heterogeneity is the rule. Inequalities of concentrations are maintained by chemical reactions and active transport. We may really say that 'coherent' behavior is the characteristic feature of biological systems.[3]

Are there two different types of physical laws? The difference of behavior is such that such a question is indeed fully legitimate.[4]

What we would like to indicate is that there are reasons to believe that these two types of behavior correspond to situations different from the point of view of thermodynamics. Broadly speaking, destruction of structures is the situation which occurs in the neighborhood of thermodynamic equilibrium. On the contrary 'creation of structures' *may* occur with specific non-linear kinetic laws of far-from-equilibrium conditions. The energy exchanged by the system with the outside world is then really transformed into structure.

The idea of associating structure with non-equilibrium is in fact rather old. I expressed it in terms of the theorem of minimum entropy production many years ago.[5] However, it is only much more recently that the detailed mechanism through which structure may originate in far-from-equilibrium conditions has

2

been understood in specific examples. Let us briefly outline the thermodynamic approach.

II THERMODYNAMICAL THEORY OF STABILITY AND STRUCTURE

To situate the problem it is useful to distinguish between two types of structures:

(a) equilibrium structures,
(b) dissipative structures.

Equilibrium structures may be maintained without any exchange of energy or matter. A crystal is a characteristic equilibrium structure. On the contrary, 'dissipative structures' are maintained only far from thermodynamical equilibrium, through exchange of energy and matter with the outside world.

Any theorem which includes the possibility of new organization of matter has to face the problem of fluctuations. As an illustration consider a typical problem in hydrodynamics: the stability of the laminar flow of a fluid. Suppose there appears a small fluctuation in the kinetic energy. How will the system react to this fluctuation? If it regresses the flow is stable; on the contrary, if it is amplified a new state of flow will be reached. As is well known from classical hydrodynamics, this will be the case if the so-called 'Reynolds number' lies beyond some critical value.

The main point is therefore the following: a new structure is always the result of an instability: it originates from a fluctuation. It is precisely such instabilities which we have to study if we want to investigate the basic question of reducibility of the two types of laws considered above. Under what conditions may the results obtained by classical thermodynamics be extrapolated to far-from-equilibrium situations? Is the increase of disorder by 'destruction of structure' still the dominant feature?

These problems have been studied by our group for some time now and I would like to summarize the answer.[6]

The second law of thermodynamics can be formulated as a 'balance equation' for entropy:

$$dS = d_eS + d_iS \quad \text{with } d_iS \geqslant 0 \qquad (1)$$

3

Here d_eS denotes the contribution of the outside world (entropy flow); and d_iS, the entropy production inside the system. The inequality $d_iS \geqslant 0$ expresses the principle that irreversible processes always produce entropy. This entropy production may be expressed in terms of the rates of irreversible processes J_ζ (chemical reaction rates, heat flow, diffusion rate . . .) and the corresponding thermodynamic forces X_ζ (chemical affinities, gradient of temperature . . .). We have:

$$\frac{d_iS}{dt} = \frac{\Sigma}{\xi} J_\zeta X_\zeta \geqslant 0 \qquad (2)$$

The entropy production is one of the basic quantities of modern thermodynamics.

But there is a second very important quantity: the 'curvature' of entropy $\delta^2 s$. For isolated systems and small fluctuations this quantity is identical to the change of entropy which appears in the basic Einstein formula for fluctuations, since the probability of a fluctuation is given by:

$$Pr \sim \exp \frac{\Delta s}{k} \sim \exp \frac{\delta^2 s}{k} \qquad (3)$$

where k is Boltzmann's constant. Indeed for an isolated system the first differential δs vanishes as the entropy is maximum at equilibrium. Therefore $\delta^2 s$ determines the size of fluctuations in isolated systems.

But the importance of $\delta^2 s$ is by no means limited to the physical situations considered by Einstein. In fact, $\delta^2 s$ is a negative definite quadratic form which determines the fluctuations for all situations which may be described in terms of a macroscopic theory with well-defined boundary conditions. The only restriction is that we have to consider small fluctuations.[7]

It is therefore very important to study the time evolution of $\delta^2 s$, as this is intimately related to the problem of regression of fluctuations and therefore, as we have seen, to the very possibility of the appearance of new dynamical states. Together with our colleagues in Brussels we have studied in great detail the general evolution laws of $\delta^2 s$. More precisely, we have established a balance equation for $\delta^2 s$ somewhat similar to the balance equation (1) for the total entropy. We do not want to go into

4

details here,[8] but we would like to mention two essential features.

To obtain instability with respect to fluctuations requires basically two conditions, firstly, some non-linear mechanism and, secondly, the maintenance of far-from-equilibrium conditions. Two types of situations are specially well suited to illustrate these conclusions.

(a) Hydrodynamics

Here the non-linearity is provided by the inertial terms which appear in the equations of motion. They are responsible for the transformation of laminar flow into turbulent flow, the appearance of convection patterns and so on . . . These examples are interesting because from the point of view of molecular behavior spontaneous convection is already a highly cooperative phenomenon in which an enormous number of molecules manifest a *coherent* behavior over a macroscopic period of time.

(b) Chemical kinetics

The variety of the laws of chemical kinetics is practically infinite. Generally they are non-linear. Also, because of the existence of an activation energy for inelastic collisions, it is easy to maintain conditions far from thermodynamic equilibrium. The study of chemical reactions in open systems therefore presents a special interest and also has a direct relevance to biological problems; so let us consider an example more in detail.

III COHERENT BEHAVIOR IN OPEN CHEMICAL SYSTEMS

Consider a system in which the following simple sequence of reactions is going on:

$$A \underset{}{\overset{1}{\rightleftharpoons}} X \underset{}{\overset{2}{\rightleftharpoons}} B \tag{4}$$
$$\underset{M}{\overset{}{\Updownarrow}} 3$$

The concentrations of the initial product A and the final

5

product B are fixed. X and M are intermediate components. This is an open chemical system exchanging matter and energy with the outside world. We expect that for given values of A and B, the concentrations of X and M will take well-defined steady state values. For example, if we assume the simple kinetic laws (we put equal to one all equilibrium and rate constants):

$$V_1 = A - X, \quad V_2 = X - B, \quad V_3 = X - M, \tag{5}$$

we easily obtain at the steady state:

$$M = X = \tfrac{1}{2}(A + B). \tag{6}$$

As a special case, (6) includes the case in which the fixed ratio A/B corresponds to thermodynamic equilibrium. Then B/A = 1 and (6) reduces to

$$M = X = A = B. \tag{7}$$

The equilibrium result (7) could of course have been directly derived using the law of mass action. We may say that in this simple case the 'thermodynamic solution' (7) may be 'extended' to the whole possible range of the constraint A/B to obtain (6). But this is not always so; so let us consider in more detail the following scheme of reactions.[9]

$$
\begin{aligned}
A &\leftrightarrows X & \text{(a)} \\
2X + Y &\leftrightarrows 3X & \text{(b)} \\
B + X &\leftrightarrows Y + D & \text{(c)} \\
X &\leftrightarrows E & \text{(d)}
\end{aligned}
\tag{8}
$$

The initial and final products are A, B, D, E. Their concentrations are maintained fixed in time. On the contrary the intermediates X and Y evolve till some asymptotic situation is reached. The overall reaction corresponding to (8) is given by:

$$A + B \leftrightarrows E + D \tag{9}$$

We may apply the thermodynamic theory we briefly summarized in the preceding paragraph to both the reaction schemes (4) and (8). In the first case it is easy to prove that fluctuations will indeed always regress, whatever the imposed values of A and B may be. This is no longer so in the second case because of the presence of the non-linear autocatalytic step (b). The production of X is increased by the very presence of X. Near thermodynamical equilibrium this is of no importance, but far-from-equilibrium fluctuations may increase in time and lead to a

6

completely new space-time organization. If we represent schematically the concentrations of one of the intermediates as a function of one of the given variables (the others having fixed constant values), we obtain a curve such as the one represented in Fig. 1.

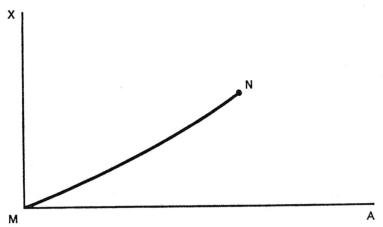

FIG. 1. Thermodynamic branch (see text)—M equilibrium point; N limit of stability.

Point M corresponds to thermodynamical equilibrium; MN is the so-called thermodynamical branch on which the steady state values of X lie. At the point N the thermodynamical branch becomes unstable. Fluctuations are then amplified. Two very interesting limiting situations may occur:

(a) The system becomes unstable with respect to perturbations homogeneous in space. In other words, the perturbations affect in the same way all points of the system. The system then leaves the steady state on the thermodynamic branch MN and reaches a well-defined final trajectory. The important point is that this trajectory corresponds to a stable periodic phenomenon. Whatever the initial state, the system approaches in time the same periodic solution, whose characteristics, such as period and amplitude, are uniquely determined. Such periodic solutions have been discovered in a different context by Poincaré[10] and are called *limit cycles*.[11] An example is indicated on Fig. 2.

It can be seen that the limit cycle reached asymptotically is indeed independent of the initial conditions.

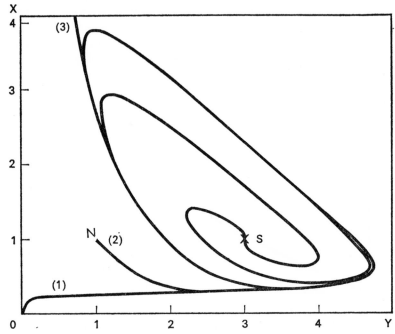

FIG. 2. Example of a limit cycle for reaction scheme (8). N is the unstable point on the thermodynamic branch.[12]

The important point is that we have here a coherent, macroscopic time organization which appears beyond the point where the thermodynamical branch becomes unstable.

(b) The same system may also become unstable with respect to inhomogeneous fluctuations affecting differently the various points of the system (for example, the fluctuations may occur only inside a small point of the volume). The conditions for instability are very similar to those in the preceding case. But now the system leaves the homogeneous state and reaches a new time-independent but non-uniform distribution. This is a 'symmetry breaking' transition as the state after the inhomogeneity is less symmetric than the state before.

Fig. 3 gives an example obtained by computer calculation. The appearance of 'structures' is striking. Diffusion is compensated by chemical reactions and the system maintains a state of low entropy. Both in the case of periodic time structures and of symmetry-breaking space transitions we have a *coherent* behavior involving a macroscopic number of molecules. The possibility of spontaneous appearance of space inhomogeneities was first noticed by Turing.[13]

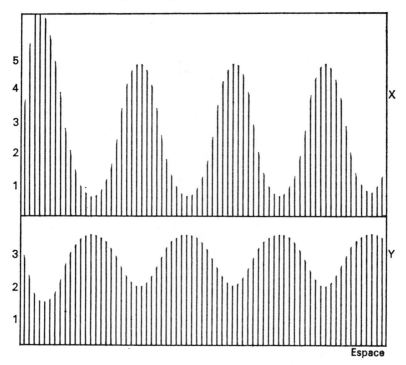

FIG. 3. Example of dissipative structure obtained from the reaction scheme (8) by computer calculation.[14]

It is interesting to notice that very recently the existence of such new 'dynamic' states of matter induced by a flow of free energy far from equilibrium has been verified experimentally.[15] Fig. 4 reproduces a photograph of the beautiful patterns which may be produced in this way by chemical reactions.

We refer to the original paper for more details about the type of reaction considered. The really exceptional interest of these experiments is to show that far-from-equilibrium macroscopic processes may indeed produce coherent behavior through a suitable amplification of molecular properties such as chemical kinetic constants by non-linear mechanisms.

9

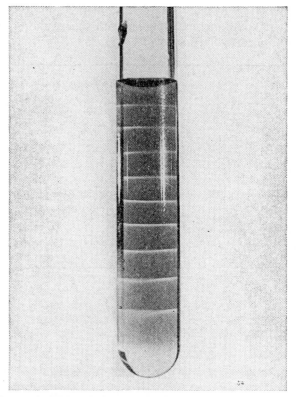

FIG. 4. Spatial patterns produced by a chemical reaction in far-from-equilibrium conditions.[16]

IV BIOLOGICAL STRUCTURES

We have seen in § 3, in concrete examples, how the variety of types of behavior may be reconciled with the unity of physical laws. We are now dealing with different situations. When we impose conditions compatible with the stability of the thermodynamical branch, we obtain essentially the usual behavior associated with an increase of 'randomness'. On the contrary, beyond this branch a completely new coherent behavior may appear.

We have here a specially striking example of the essential role of non-linearities in physical laws. It is this non-linearity which is responsible for the existence of various regimes which at first may appear as contradictory.

10

It may be asked how we can impose conditions such that the system be prevented from reaching thermodynamic equilibrium. This is essentially related to the existence of a well-defined separation of time scales between the system and the outside world, the latter evolving on a time scale much greater than that of the former. The system can then adjust itself to the outside world. This requirement can be realized experimentally. It seems also to apply (at least approximatively) to the evolution of the biosphere in our local cosmological environment. In both the 'random' regime on the thermodynamic branch and the 'coherent' regime beyond its stability, the entropy production (2) remains positive.

In *many* cases, but not always, the entropy production increases in the transition from one regime to the other.[17]

It is of course a question of much greater complexity to decide if biological structures can be associated with the type of instabilities we have considered; in other words, can biological structures be considered as open chemical systems working beyond the instability of the thermodynamical branch? Incomplete as this view may be, it has the great advantage that it may be tested experimentally. If chemical instabilities have played an important role in the origin of life, it is likely that even at present such processes are important in the basic biological cycles responsible for the maintenance of life. The data necessary to test this idea are quite incomplete. Still, some data exist, and we have analyzed them from this point of view.[18] It was concluded that the mechanism of basic multi-enzymatic reactions involved in the glycolytic cycle, the Krebs cycle and the photosynthetic cycle are such that they probably function beyond the stability limit. Also the very interesting model developed by Blumenthal, Changeux and Lefever for membrane excitability involves dissipative structures beyond thermodynamical stability.[19]

Of course this is only a first step, but it seems not impossible that the source of the space-time order of biological structures resides in the coherent behavior of physico-chemical systems beyond the thermodynamical branch.

V CONCLUDING REMARKS

An interesting aspect of the type of chemical instabilities discussed is that one has to give up the classical concept according

11

to which a physical system and the boundary conditions which are imposed upon it may be treated independently. The possibility of a dissipative structure depends on boundary conditions, but they themselves are modified by the occurrence of dissipative structures. From this point of view—again assimilating a biological system to a dissipative structure—the boundaries of a living system are far less arbitrary than for systems on the thermodynamic branch. They correspond to the limits to which the specific space-time organization characteristic of the dissipative structure extends.

Throughout this paper we have been mainly interested in the 'first' instability starting from the thermodynamic branch. This point separates two essentially different types of behavior. However it is clear that there may be an arbitrary number of instabilities following the first one.

For example, in a very interesting recent paper, E. F. Keller and L. A. Segel have shown that aggregation of slime molds may be viewed as a manifestation of instability of a uniform distribution.[20] This is an instability on a supercellular level.

Let us also quote the suggestive paper by Boyarsky[21] relating neural activity to limit cycles very similar to what we considered in § 3.

In more qualitative terms the paper by Carneiro, 'The Measurement of Cultural Development in the Ancient Near East and in Anglo-Saxon England' explicitly uses the stability concept in a historical context.[22] We are really no longer so far from the principle of the 'Instability of the Inhomogeneous' introduced by Spencer.

Clearly we perceive a whole hierarchy of structures separated by discontinuities. To make these concepts more precise, to introduce mathematical methods to distinguish, for example, between growth and instability, is an urgent task. We hope that some progress may be accomplished in the immediate future.

Concluding rather optimistically, we feel that great progress has been made towards a concrete, unified description of the macro-world. The concept of stability really reconciles the unity of laws with the existence of well-defined levels of description.

AUTHOR'S NOTE: I wish to thank my colleagues and friends Professors P. Glansdorff, G. Nicolis as well as Mr R. Lefever for many stimulating discussions.

REFERENCES

[1] H. Bergson, *L'Evolution créatrice*, Paris: Presses Universitaires de France, 1963.

[2] L. J. Henderson, *The Order of Nature*, Cambridge, Mass.: Harvard University Press, 1917. An excellent discussion of Spencer's ideas.

[3] P. A. Weiss, *Dynamics of Development*, New York and London: Academic Press, 1968.

[4] See W. Heitler, 'Der Mensch und die Naturwissenschaftliche Erkenntnis' in *Die Wissenschaft*, *116*, 1961.

[5] I. Prigogine, *Introduction to Non-Equilibrium Thermodynamics*, New York: Wiley-Interscience, third ed., 1962. Where references to the original (1945) papers are given.

[6] For more details see I. Prigogine, 'Structure, Dissipation and Life' and 'Dissipative Structures in Biological Systems' in *Theoretical Physics and Biology* (ed. M. Marois), Amsterdam: North-Holland, 1969 and 1970; P. Glansdorff and I. Prigogine, *The Thermodynamic Theory of Stability, Fluctuations and Structure*, New York: Wiley-Interscience, 1971.

[7] G. Nicolis and A. Babloyantz, 'Fluctuations in Open Systems' in *Journal of Chemical Physics*, *51*, 1969, pp. 2632-7; Glansdorff and Prigogine, *op. cit.*

[8] See Glansdorff and Prigogine, *op. cit.*

[9] R. Lefever, 'Dissipative Structures in Chemical Systems' in *Journal of Chemical Physics*, *49*, 1968, pp. 4977-8.

[10] H. Poincaré, *Les Méthodes Nouvelles de la Mécanique Céleste*, Paris: Gauthier-Villars, vol. 1, 1892 and vol. 2, 1893.

[11] See, for a detailed study, N. Minorski, *Non-Linear Oscillations*, Princeton: Van Nostrand, 1962.

[12] For details, see R. Lefever and G. Nicolis, submitted to *Journal of Theoretical Biology*, 1970.

[13] A. M. Turing, 'The Chemical Basis of Morphogenesis' in *Royal Society of London. Philosophical Transactions B*, *237*, 1952, pp. 37-72.

[14] See Lefever, *op. cit.*

[15] H. Büsse, 'A Spatial Periodic Homogeneous Chemical Reaction' in *Journal of Physical Chemistry*, *73*, 1969, p. 750; M. Herschkowitz-Kaufman, *C.R. Ac. Sc. Paris*, Ser. C., *270*, 1970, p. 1049.

[16] *Ibid.*

[17] Examples are studied in Glansdorff and Prigogine, *op. cit.*

[18] I. Prigogine, R. Lefever, A. Goldbeter, and M. Herschkowitz-Kaufman, 'Symmetry Breaking Instabilities in Biological Systems', *Nature*, *223*, 1969, pp. 913-16.

[19] R. Blumenthal, J. P. Changeux, and R. Lefever, *Comptes Rendus de l'Academie des Sciences*, Paris, 1970.

[20] E. F. Keller and L. A. Segel, *Journal of Theoretical Biology*, *26*, 1970, p. 399.

[21] L. L. Boyarsky, *Curr. mod. Biol.*, *1*, 1967, p. 39.

[22] L. Carneiro, *Trans. N.Y. Acad. Sci.*, 1969, p. 1013.

13

2

REDUCIBILITY: ANOTHER
SIDE ISSUE?

Marjorie Grene

Professor Prigogine's position represents the minimal alternative to a complete reductivism. It is 'reductive' in that it sees the laws of physics as including, in their foundation at least, the laws of organic structure, yet non-reductive in so far as it complicates physics by introducing distinctive alternatives within its scope. Such a move may prove eventually to constitute a fitting first move in the direction of a new synthesis. But those of us who are not physicists find ourselves meanwhile still confronted with a crisis in biology and in the sciences of man which demands an immediate response. Even though a thoroughgoing reductivism may be philosophically untenable as well as humanly intolerable, it may still be ideologically powerful and even in some respects conceptually resistant to the main moves so far made against it. Only a new metaphysic, as Professor Dreyfus will argue, or a new epistemology, as Professor Scott displays in his paper, will give us a radical cure for this unease. Short of such fundamental innovation, however, we may move sideways, so to speak, to alleviate the pressure of the current debate. Reductivism has been tied to a peculiar and peculiarly abstract conception of the methods of science; to liberate ourselves from this straitjacket is to free ourselves also from the prejudice which insists that all the structures studied by science are one-levelled and particulate, as we have been urged to believe. Such a move does not indeed offer any ultimate resolution of the problem, but it should open the door to more flexible conceptions both of the methodology of the sciences and of their objects.

Charles Taylor, in a paper entitled 'Mind-Body Identity: A Side Issue?',[1] argues that those who oppose mind-body identity can grant to its defendants all the concessions they desire and still maintain the theses *they* wish to defend: that, in other words, there is no substantive disagreement between the contestants in the case, and so philosophers of mind would do better to ignore

14

this alleged dispute and turn to still open and more interesting questions. A similar situation obtains, I propose to argue, with respect to the much debated question of the reduction of theories, in particular, the question of the reducibility or the irreducibility of biology to physics.

My exposition has three parts: first, an analysis of the present state of the controversy, in which we appear to find a fifth antinomy (not, however, quite antinomic in its structure); second, a suggestion of an alternative approach which, by treating the problem as a side-issue, manages to evade it; and third, a brief case-study in confirmation of the thesis of part II. No part claims any philosophical originality; the first is an attempt to sort out some of the current arguments in both sides of the issue; the second, an experiment in applying Rom Harré's theory of scientific inquiry to this particular problem; the third, an unphilosophical postscript. But I hope I can clear away some cobwebs so that we can look at more specific problems in the philosophy of biology and psychology without this impediment to our vision.

1a

First, then, about the current state of the controversy. And first, here, a preliminary adjuration which *ought* to be unnecessary; we are not dealing with the old 'mechanism'-'vitalism' quarrel. This adjuration *is* necessary, unfortunately, in view of the crude reductivism of such statements, for example, as Crick's *Of Molecules and Men*:[2] the alleged 'vitalists' he is attacking— people who hold that there is some mysterious something about living things exempt from physico-chemical laws—are scarce on the ground these days. There is of course the strange evolutionism of Teilhard de Chardin, but its import is, to say the least, ambiguous. It looks to many like a perversely mystical 'theory' of emergence; but as Huxley's enthusiasm for it indicates, it can also be taken as supporting, or at any rate as not contradicting, more orthodox biological opinion. An English version of Schubert-Soldern's *Philosophie des Lebendigen*, published in 1962 under the title *Mechanism and Vitalism*, does indeed represent a more traditional vitalist view;[3] but its quaint Aristotelianism is scarcely representative of the best anti-reductivist

15

REDUCIBILITY: ANOTHER SIDE ISSUE?

arguments by either philosophers or biologists. And on the other side, the case made by most contemporary reductivists—notably by Nagel in *The Structure of Science*[4] or by Oppenheim and Putnam in their 'Unity of Science' paper[5]—is much more temperate than Crick's. In short, the issue is not quite what it was between Loeb and Driesch in the early years of the century. Both sides nowadays agree that living systems are made of the same kind of matter as non-living, and obey physical laws; the question is only: do those laws state the sufficient as well as necessary conditions essential to the description and explanation of biological phenomena?

Leaving antiquated and extreme positions out of it, therefore, we may ask: how does the case stand nowadays for and against the reducibility of biology to physics? We can ignore chemistry, since those who hold the affirmative view consider chemistry *a fortiori* reducible—there must be *one* lowest-level set of laws into which all others are translatable and from which they can be derived.

As the arguments fly back and forth we seem to have at first sight something like a fifth Kantian antinomy. The thesis: biology *is* reducible to physics. The antithesis: biology is *not* reducible to physics.[6] Let us take, in Kantian fashion, first thesis and then antithesis as *dogma* and see what happens. The thesis in its dogmatic sense is vulnerable on two fronts, one epistemological and the other cybernetic.

The epistemological attack is an ancient one which can be stated in many forms. Let me remind you of two of them. The dogmatic reductivist asserts: Biology is reducible to physics—call this R. He will also assent to the formulation: it is true that biology is reducible to physics (it is true that R), or to the formulation: I know that biology is reducible to physics (I know that R).

What does R mean? It means that all scientific laws, including those of biology, can be translated into and are derivable from basic, universal laws of matter in motion. In effect, then, whatever one truly asserts about the world expresses, in the last analysis, some change in the configurations of matter described by physics. Usually such thinking is also particulate; that is, it is the laws of the fundamental particles of which 'matter' is composed from which the laws of macroscopic behavior are to be

16

derived. (More of that later.) It makes no difference, however, to this argument whether or not one thinks of the fundamental level as atomistic: the point is that there is just one level of existence from the laws of which all the processes of all 'higher' levels or, if you like to avoid 'level' language, of all larger systems can be derived. But the reductivist's assertion is that R is itself an event, whether of emission of sound, or making of marks on paper. Therefore, it follows, like all other processes, from the laws of the fundamental level. The alternative formulations, likewise, 'it is true that R', or 'R is true', and 'I know that R' are equally necessitated by the laws of physics. But how can a truth claim or a knowledge claim be necessitated? That it cannot be so is plain from the fact that the contradictory 'claim', non-R, R is false, I know that non-R ,enunciated by the anti-reductivist, is equally necessitated. In other words, to make a claim to knowledge is to perform an action, and, as has been argued *ad nauseam*, 'actions' demand reasons, rather than—or as well as —causes. It is the *reasons* for the act of claiming that R that constitute *evidence* for R as vs. non-R or non-R as vs. R, while both statement *and* denial are equally *caused*. Thus the reductivist's thesis, since it admits its contradictory as well as itself, contradicts itself; it can be uttered as a noise but not reasonably asserted as a claim to knowledge.

If the reductivist answers, moreover, that he must be right because, were we all mistaken in our scientific theories, natural selection would have long since exterminated us, the anti-reductivist has only to reply: here I am too! Either of us may be right, or neither, but we are equally successful. Nor is 'success' equivalent to truth: either or both of us may be guided by a useful illusion. Neither physical necessity nor practical success can give evidence for the truth or R or non-R.

This argument examines the status of the reductivist thesis in its own terms and reduces it to absurdity, much as Socrates does with the relativistic thesis of Protagoras in the *Theaetetus*. One can also show, more generally, that *any* statement presupposes the existence of more than matter in motion: that, in other words, if there is language, including physics, there must be systems (ourselves) capable of rule-governed behavior as distinct from aggregates of matter determined by physical laws (and again it makes no difference here whether the laws in question

17

are deterministic or statistical). On this question the arguments of Chomsky and Chomskyan linguists seem to me definitive.

In short, were reductivism true, knowledge would be impossible, including the knowledge that reductivism is true. And were reductivism true, language would be impossible, including the formulation of the reductivist's thesis.

The second argument depends on the claims of contemporary reductivists themselves. Since, they declare, the processes of growth and heredity have been shown to be determined by a sequence of DNA molecules, biology has already been reduced, on principle, to biochemistry; the completion of the job is routine. Granted, however, that DNA has precisely the power they claim for it, its operation demonstrates, on the contrary, that biology is *not* reducible to biochemistry (and ultimately, to physics). What makes DNA do its work is not its chemistry but the order of the bases along the DNA chain. It is this order which functions as a code to be read out by the developing organism. The laws of physics and chemistry hold, as reductivists rightly insist, universally; they are entirely unaffected by the particular linear sequence that characterizes the triplet code. Any order is possible physico-chemically; therefore physics and chemistry cannot specify *which* order will in fact succeed in functioning as a code. This argument, which appears incontrovertible, was stated by Michael Polanyi in *Science* in 1968.[7] The orderly structure of a chemical molecule, Polanyi points out, 'is due to a maximum of stability, corresponding to a minimum of potential energy.'[8] Such order, wholly determined by the laws of physics and chemistry and the boundary conditions of the system, is incapable of functioning as a code. The particular sequence of the bases on the DNA spiral, however, is not so determined. There is simply no question of energy here at all. One can say that, statistically, all sequences are equiprobable; any one, accordingly, is highly improbable, and the measure of this improbability is precisely the measure of the information it provides. Polanyi writes:

As the arrangement of a printed page is extraneous to the chemistry of the printed page, so is the base sequence in a DNA molecule extraneous to the chemical forces at work in the DNA molecule. It is this physical indeterminacy of the sequence that produces the improbability of occurrence of any particular sequence and thereby enables it to have a meaning—a meaning that has a mathematically determinate information content equal to the numerical improbability of the arrangement.[9]

We conclude, then, that the thesis contradicts itself whether as a claim to knowledge or simply as a piece of rational discourse, and the empirical evidence said most dramatically to confirm it proves in fact incompatible with it.

What about the antithesis: Biology is not reducible to physics? In other words, biology has its unique subject-matter and its unique methods which cannot on principle be translated into or derived from the laws of physics. To this statement three counter-arguments may be presented: First, there is an argument from the universality of physical laws. It runs: All material systems are governed by the laws of physics. All living systems are material. Therefore, all living systems are governed by the laws of physics. This too appears incontrovertible.

Second, moreover, there is the empirical evidence that analytical biology, which studies living systems in terms of their macromolecular parts, has in fact produced unquestionable advances of immense range and value. But the anti-reductivist, it is argued, holding as he does that it is 'wholes' not 'parts' that merit the biologist's study, would discourage such techniques and so would put a stop to research just where it is proving most fruitful.

Again historically, thirdly, science has advanced in virtue of the belief in a single scientific method and the ideal, at any rate, of a single unified body of scientific knowledge. It is the more wide-ranging hypothesis or the more powerful, i.e. more comprehensive, deductive theory that wins out in the end. Indeed, science originated from this demand for unity and cannot exist without it. As the gas laws have been reduced to the kinetic theory, so must all laws in the end be reduced to one fundamental plane. Such is the march of science! But the anti-reductivist's assertion that there are many sciences with many methods would cut off this essential *Leitmotif*. By telling him, so far and no farther, it would stifle the infant *Newton des Grashalms* in his cradle and prevent those future triumphs which might

19

have continued to flow from the all-important drive toward
unity.

1b

Here, then, is our antinomy. But is it an antinomy? In one sense,
yes: both thesis and antithesis are valuable as regulative maxims.
On the one hand, there is no end, on principle, to the knowledge
to be gained by studying the parts of living systems by bio-
chemical and physical methods, and on the other, there is no
reason to cease and every reason to continue studying complex
systems, including living systems, at their macrolevels and in
their own terms. This point is made, for example, by Robert
Rosen in a paper in *Journal of Theoretical Biology*.[10] Many
living systems, he points out—e.g. the CNS—appear 'intract-
able', i.e. irreducible to least parts from which, and from the
laws of which, those systems could be reconstructed. But it
would be folly to wait for someone to show that such systems
are, in his term, 'tractable'. They can be fruitfully studied by
exact methods in terms of systems theory. Why forbid such
investigations in the name of an abstract and unattainable
'unity of science'?

At the same time, however, there is an uncomfortable asymmetry about the two sides of our 'antinomy'. The reductivist
thesis is refutable, yet to many irresistibly convincing. The
arguments *against* reductivism are valid; yet the reductivist
position fits so smoothly into what seems, and has been for
countless scientists and philosophers, 'the world view of science'
that the counter-arguments, for all their logical power, are in
fact powerless against its authority. The arguments against the
antithesis, i.e. against anti-reductivism, on the contrary, fail
logically to refute it, and yet it is persistently difficult to maintain.

Let us look briefly at these alleged arguments. The first argument I mentioned depends on the fallacy of equivocation. 'All
material systems are governed by the laws of physics. All living
systems are material. Therefore all living systems are governed
by the laws of physics.' If we substitute 'obey' for 'are governed
by' we obtain a valid syllogism, which however, has no bearing
on the problem of reducibility. All living systems do indeed obey
the laws of physics, but without contervening the laws of

20

physics they may well obey other laws as well. To say that 'all living systems are *governed* by the laws of physics', however, while it says at least that living systems obey physical laws, seems also to say that all living systems are *explained* by them, i.e. that their regularities are functions of the laws of physics and of no other laws. That does not follow unless we know in addition that the laws of physics are the only laws there are.

The second and third 'arguments' against the antithesis, moreover, from the success of analytical biology and the power of the unity of science ideal, are not so much arguments as historical analogies. They may well serve to support the thesis as a methodological maxim, but they fail to contradict its denial as the epistemological and cybernetical arguments contradict the denial of the antithesis.

Yet the anti-reducibility position is, for many people, impossible to accept; it is too uncomfortable. Why? Because it breaks through the defenses of a simple, one-level physicalism without providing an alternative metaphysic to take its place. To think anti-reductively demands thinking in terms of hierarchical systems, of levels of reality and the like; but we don't know any longer how to think in that way—and to be told, even to *know*, that the contrary position is absurd does not in itself allow us to embrace wholeheartedly what ought to be the more reasonable alternative. For anti-reductivism is 'reasonable' only in the perverse sense that its negation is self-contradictory, not in the more substantive sense of fitting smoothly into a *Weltanschauung* in which, as people educated in the ideal of a 'scientific' world view, we can feel at home.

2a

How can we escape from this uneasy situation? There are two alternatives. One is to develop a comprehensive metaphysic consonant with the anti-reductivist view. There is one such system available, so to speak, in the twentieth century, and that is Whitehead's 'philosophy of organism', a system, however, with some grave weaknesses (notably the doctrine of 'eternal objects'). Another attempt at such a comprehensive ontology is that of David Bohm. Bohm's cosmology seems to be a kind of modern Spinozism, as rigorous, but also as obscure, as the

21

original; even were it systematically stated, as it has not yet been, it would be unlikely to convince most science-oriented philosophers.

There is another possibility, however, and that is to undercut the conception of science from which the apparent antinomy flows. This too needs a fundamental conceptual reform, but at least it evades the leap into metaphysics and works instead by taking a new look at the methods of science itself. I am referring here to Rom Harré's self-named 'Copernican revolution' in the philosophy of science, which, in what follows, I shall try to apply to the problem in hand.

2b

I can give only a very schematic account of Harré's position, partly because of the limits of space, but also because I know it only from a brief oral statement and from the manuscript of one chapter of its forthcoming book-length exposition.[11] But I hope I can say enough to show how it bears on our problem.

It has always been admitted in discussions of scientific explanation, Harré points out, that one should distinguish between the role of deductive *theories* and of theoretical *models*. Generally, however, the former have been held to be central, and the latter have been viewed as a sort of *ad hoc*, inferior addendum to them. This emphasis, he argues, is mistaken and misleading. It is chiefly through the search for and elaboration of models that science exists; compared with these activities, the so-called hypothetico-deductive method and the elaboration of formal systems of axioms or postulates and theorems deduced from them are relatively peripheral. His theory—or model—of model-building is careful and elaborate; I shall try to sketch in very rough outline its major features.

A scientific explanation, as Harré sees it, may be metaphorically described as a 'statement-picture complex' consisting of three major parts. First, there are sentences describing the puzzling phenomena needing to be explained. Second, there are sentences describing a model which might explain these phenomena, and thirdly, there are sentences belonging to other, non-problematic disciplines or sub-disciplines, or even areas of common experience, from which the model is drawn. Thus we must distinguish between the *subject* of the model and its *source*. These may be the same, but in most interesting cases are distinct. To explain the multiplication and variety of species, for example, Darwin introduced the model of Natural Selection, whose sources were the selection of favorable varieties by plant and animal breeders, the Malthusian doctrine and Paley's watch (though without its maker). In this case, as in many, the model was presented as a hypothetical mechanism which was said to stand to its subject as cause to effect. It is Natural Selection, says the Darwinian theory, which has *produced* the multiplicity of species. And if the model fits well—if, also, the sources it has drawn on are authoritative: indeed, a great many different factors may be operative here—but if, let us say, to put it broadly, the hypothetical mechanism is successful, it ceases to be hypothetical; it becomes an accepted fact. Descartes thought of the heart as a furnace; Harvey, as a pump. Descartes was wrong; it *is* a pump: it is the pumping action of the heart that *makes* the blood circulate. Such existential choices form, in Harré's view, the very heart of science: for scientists want to find out, in particular contexts, for particular ranges of phenomena, how nature really works—and sometimes, indeed, often, they succeed.

2c

The superiority of this model as an explanation of explanation leaps to the eye—but that is not my point here. The question is: what bearing has Harré's proposal on the problem of reducibility? Let us look at our problem in the light of the two concepts of scientific inquiry, the orthodox, hypothetico-deductive model, on the one hand, and, on the other, Harré's heterodoxy.

Hume's account of causal inference, he argued, in his chapter on reason in animals, was superior to its rivals because more phenomena were derivable from it: he had one theory for men *and* animals, not one for each. This demand for economy or 'simplicity' is a familiar one. Thus Reichenbach explained the superiority of general relativity, e.g. by pointing out that though we *could* keep adding additional forces to Newtonian gravity, it was much more efficient to think in more comprehensive terms, letting the inverse square law become a limiting case of a broader theory.[12] And of course that is how everybody explains the original power of the Newtonian synthesis itself. On the analogy of these examples, the ideal, therefore, is clearly *one* theory that will comprise *all* of science. This impulse to unification, we have already seen, is one of the primary objections to the anti-reductivist claim.

And, plainly, if there is to be *one* science, physics, which is the only universal science, is the one candidate. For since everything is made of matter, the laws of quantum mechanics, i.e. the fundamental laws of physics, plus initial conditions and boundary conditions, ought to give us the laws of all systems. On the other hand, the laws of special systems cannot as such be universalized. The laws of the nervous system, for example, or of the migration of peoples, cannot as such give us universal laws unless we can first break them down into, precisely, initial conditions, boundary conditions and the laws of physics—and then, those laws, the laws of nerve action or of migration, would have disappeared. So if science is to be unified, it is only through the reduction to physics that it can be unified. Such unification, the ideal of one great comprehensive theory drives us to attempt.

There is more to it than this, however: there are, and have been since Leucippus' time, a paradoxical pair of principles at work in the support of the reductivist's ideal. On the one hand, the orthodox view of scientific inquiry is presented as phenomenalism: science is shorthand for observations; theoretical constructs are conventions, enabling us to get from one stand in observation to another. And on the other hand, it is the smallest, invisible parts of things that alone are allowed to count as 'real'. Only an atomistic metaphysic, it seems, is *no* metaphysic, but a defense of phenomena *against* metaphysics. Thus when I tell my students, there are quail in my garden in the morning and robins in the afternoon, they say, nonsense, there is one gene pool in your garden in the morning and another in the afternoon. That's what you're *really* observing. In the name of scientific observation I must admit that my eyes deceive me: the real phenomena are the invisible ones demanded by the most unifying and most economical theory, the phenomena I *see* are only apparent and must be explained away.

Now I cannot indeed claim to understand this strange com-

24

bination of principles; but I think we must admit that it has long been, and continues to be, with us as a powerful intellectual force, from Lucretius, through Hobbes, to Carnap or Nagel or Oppenheim and Putnam. On the one hand, science is not allowed to tell us about the real world, only about aggregates of phenomena, and, on the other, it is only allowed to tell us about the 'primary qualities' characterizing the least parts of which all 'things' are composed: all 'reduction' of one theory to another is and must be 'microreduction'. In psychology, indeed, in associationism and C-R theory (which are still surprisingly influential, e.g. in ethology) the two motives appear to coalesce in forming the unit of the psychological, or behavioral, atom; but, again, only a metaphysical bias could so persistently misread the phenomena as such theories have to do.

Now, admittedly, the best liberation from a monolithic metaphysic would be a better metaphysic—more 'adequate', to use an old-fashioned term, to experience, both everyday and scientific. But, for one thing, as I have already confessed, I have no such to offer; and for another—and this is more important here—it is the authority of science as (mis)understood by scientists and philosophers alike that forces on us the straitjacket of a universal physics; a different—and sounder—approach to science may liberate us from this cramping restraint.

2d

What becomes of the demand for reducibility if we think of science in Harré's terms? It becomes thin air into which it vanishes.

First, Harré's approach brings back into play a maxim contrary to the unity of science ideal, a maxim which might be christened the plurality of science. This is a maxim which Kant recognized—indeed, it is the principle of the antinomies: no knowledge can be established, or even sought experimentally, about the *whole* of nature. Given our finite powers, every investigation is and must be partial and perspectival. 'Objective' knowledge works through abstraction; it must, to be manageable, neglect some features of experience in order to establish others sufficiently exact for the scientist to manipulate. The data of science, moreover, vary indefinitely and are unbounded in their scope: only some segment cut out of them can be subjected

25

to the scrutiny of any investigator or team of investigators at a given time and place. Thus on grounds both of method and content, science is partial and plural. This maxim, stressed also by Max Weber, is at least as essential to the practice of science as is the hope of unity. And it is primarily on this maxim that Harré's model of science relies. The subject of a theoretical model—the puzzling subject matter to be investigated—is always some special set of phenomena which, at some time in the development of some particular discipline, have aroused the interest of some particular investigators. Not that the ideal of unity is neglected either: for the *source* of a model may come from anywhere—as, e.g. cognitive psychology may rely on computer science; or Freudian theory on the physical concept of energy; or evolutionary theory on the work of the great cattle breeders—and so on. But this is an *open* unity, confined at the same time by the demands of a given problem. In this spirit, e.g. psychologists can use cybernetical models without thereby asserting a metaphysical dogma of 'mechanical man'. Thus Ulric Neisser writes:

> There is an important place for eventual neurological interpretations of cognitive processes . . . *but we should strive to establish a mechanism and discover its properties first.*[13]

In other words, let us look for a mechanism which might under-lie the phenomena we hope to understand, seeking wherever we may relevant sources from which to derive, first, an analogue of a possible mechanism, and then, if we are shrewd and lucky and experience bears us out, and maybe a description of the mechanism itself. There are no strict rules for this procedure, as Harré emphasizes; we have to rely on what he calls 'plausibility con-trol'. The enterprise is personal and irreducibly pluralistic, but also open-ended. Anything *may* be relevant to anything: in *this* sense, science is one, but also many.

Secondly, in so far as the demand to reduce all theories to one level springs from a phenomenalistic program, Harré's revolution cuts it off at its root. The discovery of stable mechanisms in nature, not the summary of one flat level of pure phenomena, is what science is after. The inverse square law, or the principles of evolutionary theory, or the psychology of association, or the laws of good closure, or the kinetic theory of gases, may each embrace a wide range of phenomena in its explanatory scope. And from this scope in each case, the law or theory in part derives its explanatory power. A model that modelled just *one* particular phenomenon would be admittedly of little use. But on the one hand, no such law or theory—and no law or theory—comprehends all the phenomena of every kind that any scientist wants to, or might want to, explain. And on the other hand, the explanation works in each case not just by bringing together many observations into one otherwise meaningless and conventional formula. It works by leading us to see, in the case of a particular set of puzzling phenomena, *how in fact those phenomena are produced.* I remember hearing a speaker explain, at a symposium of biology teachers ten or twelve years ago, in the early days of DNA-RNA research, that what biochemists were doing was to ask 'what is the genetic mechanism that in fact produces the effects which we see?' This is a case not of looking for a sentence or sentences from which the phenomena in question can be deduced, but of seeking the then unknown processes in nature which determine—in the sense of having the power to produce—certain perceptible effects.

Indeed, it is strange that the orthodox theory of explanation, which is phenomenalistic in intent, supposes itself also to be causal. To predict one darned thing after another is not in any sense to say *why* one follows the other. By themselves, a sequence of phenomena can give at most constant conjunction, not necessary connection. That is just what Hume discovered. What Humean 'necessary connection' adds to constant conjunction is simply the force of habit, or as Russell calls it, 'animal inference'. If B has always followed A, I may come, on A's occurrence, to expect B, but such a sequence, on its own, is not explanatory: only the fitting of both A and B into a rational context enables one to say, in the light of C, when A, then B. Indeed, it has never been possible, in all honesty, to give a reasonable account of scientific method in pure phenomenalist terms. Even Hempel and Oppenheim, in their famous paper on explanation, admit that in addition to the observables in the case, we must have a law-like statement, from which they 'follow', and even (apologetically) one which is 'true'.[14] And Hempel in 'The Theoretician's Dilemma' is still wrestling with this concession.[15]

27

Admit, on the contrary, that scientists are trying, not to tie phenomena together into convenient bundles, but to look for the hidden mechanisms that produce them, and you are rid of the anomalies of the phenomenalist position—and at the same time of one of the prime motives for demanding universal reduction. For again, the central task of science in Harréan terms is the imaginative construction of theoretical models which suggest ways in which particular sets of phenomena may be *produced*. Such models are apposite for, and succeed in explaining, in the first instance, the phenomenon they were intended to explain— and perhaps, if they are powerful enough, others as well: but not *everything*. To find that the heart pumps blood explains a lot about the circulation but not, e.g. the action of the liver (nor even for that matter of the lungs—which was still a mystery to Harvey). To find that the anopheles mosquito carries *plasmodium malariae* explains how malaria is contracted, but not the cause of cancer. When we look at science from this perspective, the overabstract ideal of one unified system drops away, and with it the demand that all sciences be reduced to physics—and *a fortiori*, the need to combat that demand.

By the same token, finally, the dogma of microreduction lets go its stranglehold. On the model-model of scientific method, as we may call it, we can see both why microreduction is so powerful a tool of scientific advance, and why it has not been and need not be the single and exclusive technique for relating one science to another. Every model, we have seen, models its subject by drawing on some source, usually distinct from that subject. Such a model *may* just give us a new way of thinking about the subject (as light waves do for color), but often the model is proposed as a hypothetical mechanism which, if it exists, bears a causal relation to the subject as its effect. Dalton's atomic theory itself was such a hypothetical mechanism which has come, in a form severely modified by comparison with his own version, to be accepted as real. However intricate the modern 'atom', on the one hand, and however justified, on the other, is the movement away from particulate thinking in contemporary physics, the fact remains that for ordinary purposes common salt is correctly described as $NaCl$ or water as H_2O (not HO as Dalton thought). There was substantial resistance to Dalton's theory as late as sixty years ago—that's another fascinating story which should

28

be told in Harréan terms; the history of atomism is far from the triumphal progress Reichenbach supposed it to be. But let that slipshod remark suffice here; the point is simply that the decision has been made, there *are* atoms, not indeed as ultimate indivisibles, but as units of chemical reaction, and many properties of familiar compounds are successfully explained in these terms. Given this fact, plus the natural tendency of many minds (whatever the reason) to think of explanation as analysis, plus the association of corpuscular thinking with such names as Newton and Boyle, it becomes habitual to draw one's models for *other* sciences, more or less directly, from the successful principles of atomism. See Nagel's favorite case, the kinetic theory of gases.[16] See, in reliance on a more remote analogy, the cell theory, or the theory of the gene. One may even be tempted to assert, with Gillispie, that all advances in science are advances to, and in, particulate thinking, and all moves away from such thinking retrogressions.[17]

But that would be a serious error. Not only is it being impressively argued in some quarters that particulate thinking has partly been, and needs to be wholly, replaced in physics.[18] The reliance on atomism as a source of theoretical models has never been as exclusive or as complete as its defendants assume. Oppenheim and Putnam, for example, suggest in their 'Unity of Science' paper six levels of microreduction, of which the first three are: communities to living organisms to cells.[19] This is an oversimplification extreme to the point of absurdity. True, communities are made up of individuals; there is no existent superindividual such as Teilhard envisaged with his 'noosphere'. Yet ecology as the study of animal and plant communities is not a summation of the facts of individual behavior. Take a work like Fraenkel and Gunn's *Orientation of Animals*, which is explicitly 'reductivist' in its import.[20] It is precisely the emphasis on individuals—who might be suspected, heaven forbid, of 'purposive behavior'—that these authors wish to avoid. A traffic jam, they point out, is not explained through any given drivers, or any group of drivers, trying to get to work; it is the overall laws of the collective that explain the situation, despite, not because of, the behavior of each individual. In general, I think it may be safely said, ecology draws its models from many sources: from thermodynamics, from statistics, from chemical engineering, from computer science, not by any means wholly or even primarily from the laws governing the community's parts. In particular, the theory of natural selection, although strongly influenced in our time by the particulate theory of the gene, constantly and necessarily escapes reductivist thinking. Darwin's original model, to begin with, by showing how predator-prey relations and more generally organism-environment relations generate increased adaptation to new environments, typically exhibits *hierarchical, not reductive* thinking. A hierarchy (I am following here Howard Pattee's description) is first a collection of elements such that the elements are subject to the laws peculiar to their level; while, secondly, the interactions between them produce patterns imposing restraints upon those very elements; restraints, thirdly, which must operate with a certain reliability if the hierarchy is to survive.[21] Thus even though there are no elements in the collection other than individual organisms and their physical as well as organic environments—there are only, for example, bees, clover, cats, mice and spinsters in Darwin's famous example—the interaction between these constrains the operation of the elements themselves in a way which from the study of the elements at their own level we could neither have predicted nor understood. Or to put it in the fashion beloved of contemporary Darwinians, only thinking in terms of populations, *not* individuals, allows us to formulate evolutionary theory. And if evolutionary theory is the proper framework of biology, as its proponents maintain, then biology is typically macro—not micro—reductive, or better anti-reductive in its chief import. Indeed, so powerful, because of its central role in this central theory, is the concept of 'population' that it can itself serve in turn as a source for other models: as in the study, through computer techniques, of 'populations' of muscle cells. Such thinking, like population-genetical theorizing in terms of gene pools, has of course the advantage of *appearing* also to be particulate and so acquiring some of the prestige of atomism: for it works in terms of collections of bits. Yet it is at the same time, and fundamentally, hierarchical thinking in so far as it is the laws of the *collection*, not of its elements, which are being investigated.

With respect to the next alleged reductive level, organisms and cells, the oversimplicity of Oppenheim and Putnam's hypothesis

30

is even more apparent. As formulated, it has a quaintly nineteenth-century ring; but suppose we put it instead in Crickian terms, in terms of the reduction of biology to a molecular science, substituting the DNA molecule for the cell. Every molecule can then be studied in terms of physics and chemistry. True; there is no special 'organic matter'. But to function in such a way as to produce biological structures, DNA molecules, or any other molecules, must be programmed. And a programmed system, again, is hierarchical. It can be made, predicted or understood only in terms of engineering principles as well as of physics and chemistry. It is, as Polanyi calls it, a system with dual control. This has been argued conclusively not only in the paper I quoted earlier, but also, for example (if in a different spirit), by Richard Gregory in a paper on 'The Brain as an Engineering Problem'[22] or by Longuet-Higgins in Waddington's Theoretical Biology series.[23] Thanks to the prestige of reductivism, it is a difficult argument to grasp, and I shall not attempt to restate or reinforce it here. Let my report of the code argument, which is a corollary of it, serve as its representation. I only want again to point out that in Harré's terms this argument, otherwise so hard to swallow, presents no difficulty to our intellectual digestions. We are entirely at liberty to draw our models whence we please: why not from cybernetics or general systems theory if from such sources we acquire plausible suggestions for a mechanism which, if correctly guessed at, would in fact 'produce the effects that we see'? To define living systems, with Longuet-Higgins, as machines capable of improving their own programs may sound to 'organismic' biologists like one more reductivist slogan. Yet it says in effect: look to engineering —to blueprints and operational principles—*not* to chemistry and physics—for the sources of your theoretical models in biology, much as Darwin drew on the work of sheep breeders and pigeon fanciers as a source for Natural Selection. The concept of genetical selection works of course (more or *less* successfully), by combining atomic and selectional sources, and much bio-chemical research works, admittedly, by relying on particulate thinking—and hence on the success first of atomism and then of quantum mechanics—as its principal inspiration. But there is no reason why any discipline should draw all its models from one source. 'Contemporary biology', Robert Rosen remarks in the

31

paper already mentioned, is still 'dominated by the viewpoint that a total understanding of biological activity is to be found in the systematic physico-chemical fractionation of organisms, and the intensive study of the resulting fractions by means of the standard techniques of physics and chemistry.'[24] But, he argues, such techniques of fragmentation have limits as well as strengths. Though reduction is never impossible *a priori* in any given case, what it produces is often artifact, so that the properties of the fractions of a system studied 'give no information at all concerning . . . the overall system'[25] on which it was thought to bear. In such cases, in other words, to put it in Harréan terms, analytical techniques produce models, drawn, indeed, from an impeccable *source* but with limited if any bearing on their subject, models, moreover, which may well fail to give us information about their subject, precisely because they are of our own making; as natural mechanisms, they do not exist. True, that is no reason to abandon microreductive models, but it *is* good reason to supplement them with models drawn from other sources. Indeed, Rosen argues, such alternatives, by suggesting new questions, may shed important light on physics itself. In short, once one looks at scientific inquiry pragmatically and pluralistically, as Harré suggests, as an effort to solve particular problems by seeking wherever one plausibly can for hypothetical mechanisms that might explain them, there is no compulsion to look always to one source—and that a source which often supplies over-abstract and artificial analogies. It is true, of course, as Rosen concludes, that the analytical approach 'has already told us much that we wish to know about the intimate details of biological processes, and promises to tell us much more in the future.'[26] At the same time, the very achievements of this method tend to generate overconfidence in its power. 'Many important aspects of biological activity,' Rosen argues, 'are certain to be refractory to reductionist techniques, and must be treated holistically and relationally.'[27] Moreover, these aspects, he believes, 'raise general methodological and system theoretic questions of the greatest interest.'[28] Thus it is important to the development of 'a true theoretical biology' to understand the limitations of analytical methods as well as their strengths.[29] Reductivist or analytical *techniques*, in other words, have been and will be of great heuristic value; the same is true, however, of systemic or relational techniques as well. Only an outworn and over-abstract theory of theories compels us wholly to exclude the second in favor of the first.

3

So much for my general argument. Let me conclude, then, by mentioning an example which strikingly supports my thesis: the study of perception, and in particular J. J. Gibson's *The Senses Considered as Perceptual Systems.*[30]

I have often wondered why eighteenth-century philosophers were so convinced that there must be minimal sensibles. Partly of course through the influence of the 'new mechanical philosophy', which in turn had been influenced by the empiricist transmutation of the Cartesian clear and distinct idea. But the good Bishop Berkeley, for instance, who was no great admirer of the new science, filled his commonplace book with the record of his search for the minimum visible, the minimum audible. Only through describing the aggregation of such minima, it was held, could one construct a true account of perception; only through an aggregation of sensations do we perceive. I need scarcely reiterate here the commonplace that the distinction between elementary recountable sensations and perceptions somehow put together out of them, whether by 'association' or 'unconscious inference', dominated psychology at least until the advent of the Gestalt school, and in many quarters even longer.

Now along comes Gibson and tells us that such elementary sensations don't exist—well, hardly ever. The senses, in their more interesting and 'normal' role, are not purveyors of sensations, but detection systems through which organisms sometimes passively receive, but more frequently and significantly act to obtain information about their environment.

How do the old and the new theories look in Harréan terms? The subject-matter, the puzzling phenomenon to be investigated, is the question: how we use our senses to find out about the world. The hypothetical mechanism traditionally suggested was based on a building brick model; its sources were presumably the prestige of atomic thinking in physics, the successes of technology and the like. And so convincing was this hypothetical mechanism in its day that the bricks it needed were taken as facts. There *must* be least sensations (in philosophical parlance: sense data), so there *are*. Or in terms of physicalism or classical behaviorism, there must be least units of the CNS, reflexes, out of which behavior is constructed, so there are. In the case of visual perception, moreover, there was one given, or apparent given: the visible image at the back of the ox's eye. Here it was; Descartes himself had seen it. Out of such items, therefore, visual perception must be built. And if the image exists in this case, so must it in others. As a source for interpreting the retinal image, further, there is physical optics: a branch of the one sacrosanct universal science. The statement-picture-complex was authoritative; and the existential choices it demanded, compelling.

Such choices, however, are not necessary. Other experimental work (Gibson cites Köhler, Michotte and Johannsen, for example) and the principles of other disciplines (evolutionary biology and ecology, for instance; perhaps also General Systems Theory and Information Theory) may suggest a very different hypothetical mechanism or even a set of hypothetical mechanisms, which, if they prove acceptable, entail very different existential choices—and suggest also the development of other disciplines which may in their turn serve as the source for further models.

I cannot fairly paraphrase Gibson's argument here, and I hope I need not. Let us take the hypothetical mechanism he proposes for vision as summarized in his chart of the perceptual systems.[31] The essential opposition to traditional theories appears most plainly under the column 'Stimuli available'. These are, in his view, 'the varieties of structure in ambient light'. These, he holds, are acted on by the 'ocular mechanism', which includes 'eyes, with intrinsic and extrinsic eye muscles, as related to the vestibular organs, the head and the whole body' to provide information about 'everything that can be specified by the variables of optical structure (information about objects, animals, motions, events and places)'.[32] The sources for this hypothetical mechanism, I have suggested, are evolutionary theory and ecology. It needs to be substantiated, its author admits, by the development of what he calls 'ecological optics', and this in turn has as its sources 'parts of physical optics, illumination engineering (again) ecology and perspective geometry',[33] all 'respectable'

MARJORIE GRENE

fields to which an experimental innovator may reasonably look for support. And of course the parallel hypothetical mechanisms for the other perceptual systems will also confirm and be confirmed by the acceptance of the visual system. Finally, the theory entails predictions[34] capable of experimental testing, which will strengthen or weaken the case for its acceptance and the acceptance of the existential choices which it carries with it. These include, for example, the denial of sensations as universally existent, the acceptance of immediate contact with the external world, the acceptance of the structures of ambient light as real aspects of the natural world.

These are all revolutionary changes; but why not? In terms of Harré's theory of scientific method, there is no one impeccable and universal source from which the scientist must draw his models. It is high time that our obeisance to evolutionary theory and to the importance of organism-environment relations should really direct our thinking and allow us to make more sense of the senses than the search for sensory atoms permitted. Here as elsewhere, reductivist techniques have been and may yet (in their proper place) prove fruitful, but here as elsewhere they often produce artifact.

REFERENCES

[1] C. Taylor 'Mind-Body Identity: A Side Issue?' in *Philosophical Review*, 76, 1967, pp. 201–13.
[2] F. Crick, *Of Molecules and Men*: University of Washington Press, 1966.
[3] R. Schubert-Soldern, *Mechanism and Vitalism* (tr. C. E. Robin): University of Notre Dame, 1962.
[4] E. Nagel, *The Structure of Science*, New York: Harcourt, Brace & World, 1961.
[5] P. Oppenheim and H. Putnam, 'Unity of Science as a Working Hypothesis' in *Minnesota Studies in Philosophy of Science*, II, *Concepts, Theories, and the Mind-Body Problem* (eds H. Feigl, M. Scriven and G. Maxwell): University of Minnesota Press, 1963, pp. 3–36.
[6] Kant of course held that there would not be a Newton of a blade of grass; the question for him was not arguable. Had he thought it arguable, however, he would, one supposes, have reversed the two theses, taking reducibility, with its 'materialist' and anti-theistic implications, as antithesis and the more conservative alternative as thesis. But not only can I say what I want to more easily if I take it the other way around—I would also suggest that if in our situation any 'religious' bias comes into play, it is not so much the opposition of religion to science as the religion *of* science that is involved. What used to be the 'new

35

corpuscular philosophy' has become the faith of the orthodox, which a more pluralistic conception of reality appears to challenge.

[7] M. Polanyi, 'Life's Irreducible Structure' in *Science, 160,* 1968, pp. 1308–12. Essentially the same argument has been stated, for example, by David Hawkins in *The Nature of Language,* London: W. H. Freeman, 1964, by H. Pattee in *Towards a Theoretical Biology,* I and II (ed. C. H. Waddington): Edinburgh University Press, 1968 and 1969, respectively; a similar argument is stated by C. P. Raven in 'The Formalization of Finality', *Folia Biotheoretica B, 5,* 1960, pp. 1–8.
[8] Polanyi, *op. cit.,* p. 1309.
[9] *Loc. cit.*
[10] R. Rosen, 'Some Comments on the Physico-Chemical Description of Biological Activity' in *Journal of Theoretical Biology, 18,* 1968, pp. 380–6.
[11] R. Harré, *Scientific Principles in Thinking:* Oxford University Press, 1970.
[12] *Cf.* H. Reichenbach, *The Philosophy of Space and Time,* New York: Dover, 1958.
[13] U. Neisser, *Cognitive Psychology,* New York: Appleton-Century-Crofts, 1966, p. 20.
[14] C. Hempel and P. Oppenheim, 'Studies in the Logic of Explanation' in *Philosophy of Science, 15,* 1948, pp. 135–75, p. 137; this also appeared in *The Structure of Scientific Thought* (ed. E. H. Madden), Boston: Houghton-Mifflin, 1960, pp. 19–29.
[15] C. Hempel, 'The Theoretician's Dilemma' in *Minnesota Studies in Philosophy of Science,* II, *Concepts, Theories and the Mind-Body Problem* (eds H. Feigl, M. Scriven and G. Maxwell): University of Minnesota Press, 1963, pp. 37–98.
[16] Nagel, *op. cit.,* pp. 338–45.
[17] C.C. Gillispie, *The Edge of Objectivity:* Princeton University Press, 1960.
[18] *Cf., e.g.,* J. M. Burgers, *Experience and Conceptual Activity,* Cambridge, Massachusetts: M.I.T. Press, 1965, and M. Čapek, *Philosophical Impact of Contemporary Physics,* Princeton, New Jersey: Van Nostrand Press, 1961.
[19] Oppenheim and Putnam, *op. cit.,* p. 9.
[20] G. S. Fraenkel and D. L. Gunn, *Orientation of Animals,* Oxford: Clarendon Press, 1940.
[21] *Cf.* H. Pattee, 'Physical Problems of Heredity and Evolution' in *Towards a Theoretical Biology,* II (ed. C. H. Waddington): Edinburgh University Press, 1969, pp. 227–32.
[22] R. L. Gregory, 'The Brain as an Engineering Problem' in *Current Problems in Animal Behaviour* (eds W. H. Thorpe and O. L. Zangwill): Cambridge University Press, 1961, pp. 307–30.
[23] C. Longuet-Higgins, 'What Biology is About' in *Towards a Theoretical Biology,* II (ed. C. H. Waddington): Edinburgh University Press, 1969, pp. 227–32.
[24] Rosen, *op. cit.,* p. 380.
[25] *Ibid.,* p. 386.

[26] *Loc. cit.*
[27] *Loc. cit.*
[28] *Loc. cit.*
[29] *Loc. cit.*
[30] J. J. Gibson, *The Senses Considered as Perceptual Systems*, Boston: Houghton-Mifflin, 1966.
[31] *Ibid.*, Table 1, p. 50.
[32] All of the above are taken from Gibson's Table 1, *loc. cit.*
[33] *Ibid.*, pp. 221–2.
[34] *Ibid.*, see for example p. 215 on perception of the blackness of a surface with varying illumination, depth, information and so on.

3

HOW IS MECHANISM CONCEIVABLE?

Charles Taylor

The previous essay, in its references to evolutionary theory and to engineering principles, for instance, accepts the thesis that 'mechanisms' are non-reduced and indeed irreducible structures. They are always two-levelled. But as Professor Taylor points out in the course of his argument, the term 'mechanism' is ambiguous. It denotes both (1) machinery, mechanisms, which need both physics and engineering (or physiology) for their explication, and (2) a conception of nature as wholly governed by mechanical laws, i.e. one-level laws of matter-in-motion, as in the 'new mechanical philosophy' of Newton and Boyle. Professor Taylor's examination of 'mechanism' concerns the latter concept. He is asking, in particular, about the explanation of human action, which is intentional, in terms of neurological processes, which are 'mechanically' caused and without intentional import. His response to the reductivist is, like the one that has preceded it, partial and tentative. He sees 'mechanism' as, indeed, within limits conceivable, yet confined by the reasonable demands of human self-knowledge to harmless and even useful bounds.

Must a neurophysiological account of human behaviour be a mechanist one? This is the question I would like to address myself to in this paper.

The common sense of our age, informed to some degree by the scientific tradition, seems to fall naturally into a Kantian antinomy on this question (as Marjorie Grene has pointed out);[1] that is, both the thesis and the antithesis seem to be grounded in solid argument. On one hand, it appears natural to proceed on the assumption that there is no upper limit to our ability to account for the functioning of ourselves and other animate organisms in terms of body chemistry and neurophysiology, and it is equally natural to assume that such accounts will be mechanistic—particularly in view of the sterility of rival approaches, such as vitalism. It even seems plausible to argue that

38

'mechanistic explanation' is a pleonasm, for any other kind of account appears rather to sidestep the problems of explanation; it does not, in other words, increase our ability to predict and control the phenomena as explanations should.

On the other hand, common sense is alarmed by the prospect of a complete mechanistic account of behaviour; not just alarmed practically, because of the unscrupulous use to which this knowledge might be put, but alarmed metaphysically, if I may use this term, because of what such an explanation would show about us. One of the commonest expressions of this concern centres in the issue of determinism, and the sense that somehow a complete mechanistic explanation would radically undermine our whole complex of notions which centre around freedom and moral responsibility.

But before going on to look at the arguments here it would be well to try to define more closely what distinguishes a mechanistic explanation and makes it both so plausible and threatening.

The features we are looking for are best brought out by contrast with our ordinary way of talking about and explaining our behaviour at the everyday level. This talk has two features which mechanistic explanation does away with: first, it is teleological, that is, it describes our behaviour in terms of purpose, bent, desire, and other such concepts; second, it is 'intentional', that is, it constantly takes account of the meaning of things, environment and self, for the agent. A further word about these two features might help here. In saying that our talk is teleological, I am pointing to the fact, for instance, that our characterization of action in ordinary speech is usually in terms of the purpose sought in the action, so that we tend to withdraw or at least modify action ascriptions if we find that we were mistaken about the purpose. But this is not all: crucially, our explanations in ordinary language terminate with the invocation of a purpose, desire, or feeling, itself partly defined by what it disposes us to do—in short, our explanations terminate with a view of the agent as disposed to behave in a certain way, or as inclined to react in a certain way. We explain what someone does typically by sentences like these: 'he aims to become President', 'he loves her very much', 'he was terrified of meeting her again', 'that was a very provoking remark' (sc. a remark which tends to anger the person addressed), and so on. Hence the background to explanation in ordinary life is a picture of the agent as the subject of goals, desires, inclinations, susceptibilities of certain kinds. We are usually satisfied with an explanation when it relates the behaviour to be explained to one of the pictures of an agent which we accept as 'normal' in our civilization—for instance, in our case, when we explain someone's following some training by his aim to get ahead. Of course, these pictures of the normal agent vary from civilization to civilization, and sometimes from milieu to milieu within a society, which makes them very unsatisfactory in a scientific context.

The implications of our talk being intentional are not just that we distinguish between the situation and agent as they are *simpliciter* and as they are for the agent, but also that mediating propositions concerning what can loosely be called relations of meaning enter into our explanations. Suppose we are puzzled by why my interlocutor suddenly left the room, slamming the door behind him. It seems that he was angry at what I said; but why? The answer will come by filling in something of the background of his life and/or how he sees and feels about things (and in this context these two cannot be separated). We feel we understand when, for instance, we see that granted this background, and hence this way of seeing/feeling about things, what I said was insulting, or could be mistaken for an insult. Perhaps it sounded as though I was mimicking the accent of his region, or perhaps I showed insensitivity to a form of suffering which he has massively undergone.

In filling in this background we show how what I said could have the meaning of an insult, or an expression of contempt for him. What is crucial here is a relation of meaning: saying 'P' here in this way and at this time is insulting because it is (taken for) an expression of contempt; and as always, its having this meaning is contingent on its being embedded in a complex of other relations of meaning—on that regional accent's betokening for some an obtuseness or lack of sophistication, on that suffering's being for my interlocutor constitutive of his own identity and sense of worth, and so on.

Now these two features allow us to see more clearly both sides of the antinomy. On one hand, the model of explanation in natural science which has been applied in physiology has no place for ascriptions of bent or inclination; at the same time, it shies away from meaning relations as from the plague. For these can only be made clear, as we saw, against the background of a whole web of meaning, and this kind of thing is notoriously difficult to make clear in an unambiguous way and inter-subjectively. Thus it would appear that the neurophysiological explanation to which we can ascribe no upper limit must continue to eschew these features and, hence, be mechanistic in the way I would like to define it here.

But on the other hand, these features are an essential part of our notion of ourselves. If we can give a complete mechanistic explanation of our behaviour and feeling, then, we feel obscurely, this will amount to saying that these features are not essential after all. But surely, our having goals is essentially involved in our being creatures capable of freedom and responsibility, and our very existence as talking animals seems inconceivable unless our behaviour is partly determined by relations of meaning.

We are thus torn apart by the warring tendencies of our intellect. It is at this point that philosophy often enters as a peacemaker and tries to convince us that there is really no question of incompatibility here. It is perhaps always unfair to plant the straw men one wants to attack in someone else's garden, but it seems to me that among recent Anglo-Saxon philosophers, Ryle[2] and Melden[3] have presented variants of this position. The argument seems to be something like this: our ordinary account of behaviour and the scientific explanation of it in neurophysiological terms cannot clash because they are talking about different things, and moreover serve quite different purposes. Our ordinary account characterizes our behaviour as action, while a mechanistic account is interested in explaining it *qua* movement. The latter account aims to lay bare the causes of this movement, while our explanation of action in ordinary terms is not causal at all: it explains in the sense of filling in the background, of giving further information about what kind of behaviour it is.

I think all such attempts to make peace by keeping the combatants in separate rooms are doomed to failure. The basic problem is that our ordinary accounts of action are causal in a perfectly straightforward sense, even if they are not mechanistic. When I know that someone is doing what he is doing because he

41

has goal G, I am able to predict and also in certain circumstances affect the course of his behaviour in a way I couldn't before. To know the purposes, desires, feelings or whatever, that condition people's behaviour is to know the causal background of their actions, and hence to know better what would alter it, or deflect it, what is likely to happen in future under what circumstances, etc. In short, our ordinary accounts licence subjunctive and counter-factual conditionals just as mechanistic causal accounts do. Moreover, the fact that the two accounts use different descriptive languages, that of action and movement respectively, doesn't allow us to conclude that they are talking about different things in any relevant sense, for identity-relations can easily be mapped between the two ranges of things described.

But two such causal accounts, i.e. accounts which generate conditionals, are automatically potential rivals. Let us say that we explain a given stretch of behaviour in the ordinary way as action and also by some mechanistic physiological explanation as movement. *Ex hypothesi*, the *explicanda* in these two accounts are compatible, since these represent two descriptions of the same behaviour which has in fact occurred. But this does not mean that the two accounts are compatible; for both generate conditionals, and these have to be compatible at every point if the two explanations are to be judged so. Thus to explain the behaviour by neurophysiological state P_1 is to say, in terms of the mechanistic theory, that it would not have occurred, or would have occurred in modified form, if the state had been P_2. But this state P_2 may correspond to a motivational state which would be described in ordinary terms as G_b. Assuming that we originally explained the behaviour as action in terms of G_a, then the substitution of G_b for G_a would have to have the same consequences in cancelling and modifying the behaviour as the shift from P_1 to P_2. But supposing our explanation in terms of G_a were such that it would lead us to predict that the shift to G_b would intensify the behaviour, or alter it in some other way (while the shift from P_1 to P_2 would entail no parallel prediction)? In this case the two explanations could not both be true; typically we would decide between them by bringing about P_2-G_b and seeing what happened.

Two such accounts of the same events are thus potential rivals in the sense that they each trail a cluster of conditionals that may clash at some point. It is because of already recognized clashes of this kind that we accept that certain physiological explanations rule out certain motivational ones. To class some behaviour as reflex is to take it right out of the realm of purposive explanations, so that we cease to count it as action at all. This is so because a reflex in this sense is behaviour which can be produced by certain conditions in complete independence of the purposes of the agent. We know therefore in advance for any and every purposive explanation that some of its conditionals will be false, i.e. those which delineate the circumstances in which the action will not come about.

But this is not to say that causal accounts of the same phenomena are always rivals. On the contrary, they can be compatible, but this is only so when they are systematically related in some way. For each account generates an indefinite number of conditionals. It is not just enough that there is no clash for a given list of such conditionals; conflict must be absent over the whole non-finitely, delimitable range. In other words, it must be impossible to generate a conditional from one which will put it into conflict with the other. But this can be so only if there is some systematic relationship between the two.

Of course, there could be two unrelated laws stating necessary conditions, where both had to be met to provide a sufficient condition, and there could be two unrelated laws stating sufficient conditions where neither is necessary. But one could not state a sufficient and the other a necessary condition without there being some relation between the two. Now to focus on our problem, it is clear that our hypothetical complete mechanistic explanation in neurophysiological terms would provide us with both necessary and sufficient conditions for all our behaviour. ('Sufficient' here means 'sufficient within the system'; we take for granted that a whole host of external conditions for the normal functioning of the organism—enough air, absence of cosmic catastrophe, temperatures between certain limits, and so on—is met.) And with our ordinary explanations too, we frequently offer—in a quite unsystematic way, it is true—necessary and/or sufficient conditions (where 'sufficient' has the same restrictions as above).

Hence it would follow that these two accounts are potential rivals and that we cannot see them as coexisting happily in two unrelated universes of discourse. But then the threat of an antinomy returns. On one hand, the bent of our scientific culture seems to point us toward an eventual complete mechanistic account of behaviour; on the other hand, as a potential rival, this account could clash with and hence brand as erroneous the whole range of our ordinary explanations which we give and accept in everyday life. But this, quite apart from being disquieting, is unthinkable.

This last point requires, perhaps, further comment. Why should a clash of this kind be unthinkable? If it should arise, why couldn't we just reject our ordinary view in favour of the 'scientifically' better-grounded one? Is this not what has happened in all other spheres where scientific enquiry has taken us beyond common sense? After all, we have not privileged the ordinary teleological view of inanimate object behaviour which earlier attempts at physics enshrined. Why should we be more tender with animate behaviour?

The answer to this is an argument which seems to have no parallel elsewhere in philosophy. It is just that this supposition is too preposterous to be believed. For we are not talking here about the rejection of this or that old-wives' tale about behaviour, such as that rhino horn increases sexual desire. If all efficient-causal physiological explanation had the same logical relation to our ordinary account by motive as has the explanation in terms of reflexes, we would have to say that no part of our behaviour deserved the name 'action', that our entire vocabulary with the distinctions it marks had been systematically inapplicable, that the connections we experience between Xing and the desire to X were without foundation, and so on. And this is just too preposterous to swallow.

The difficulty here springs from the fact that our descriptive language for behaviour and feeling is closely tied to a certain sort of explanation. In other words, it is a peculiarity of the language with which we describe our behaviour and feelings that it characterizes these as susceptible of explanation of a certain sort. To characterize something as action in a certain context is to say that it is explicable by goals or inclinations, and to give a particular action-description is to narrow the range of acceptable goals or inclinations which can be invoked. To characterize a feeling by a certain emotion term is to say that it is linked to a certain situation which is seen as being of a certain type, *viz.* the appropriate object of this emotion. If I am feeling guilt, then it is over some wrong of which I am guilty; if I cannot see an adequate object in the putative cause, then I search further in my unconscious feelings to see what (perhaps highly irrational) sense of wrong is at the root of this.

Now I may be mistaken, this may not be guilt that I feel. But it is not possible to accept the proposition that we are always mistaken, that a concept of this kind has no application at all. Similarly we are often wrong in our action-descriptions, but we cannot claim that all our action descriptions are misplaced on the grounds that all behaviour is explicable by the type of physiological efficient-causal explanation, which like that by reflexes rules action out. This 'cannot' does not repose on any argument, but simply on the impossibility of believing that we have been talking nonsense all these millennia.

We can thus imagine hypothetical mechanistic explanations which we would be led to reject out of hand because they clashed with our ordinary account in such a way as to make nonsense of all our current vocabulary. In order to avoid this consequence, we must conceive any mechanistic explanation as systematically related to our ordinary account, and hence as *grosso modo* avoiding rivalry with it.

And in fact the model of this coordination is readily available: it is that of the reduction of one theory or set of laws to another in the sciences. An example of this is offered by the reduction of the Boyle-Charles law, and also various phenomena of thermodynamics, to a more basic explanation in terms of the kinetic theory of gases. In this case, two explanations are coordinated in that once we can establish connections between descriptions of states in the languages of both theories (meeting Nagel's 'conditions of connectability') we can derive the laws of the less basic system from those of the more basic together with those connecting correlations (hence meeting Nagel's 'conditions of derivability').[4]

We can call one system more basic than another when the two are coordinated in this way: when one has a broader application than the other, or itself stems from the specification of laws which are broader in application, so that the conditions of the less basic laws' holding can be stated in the more basic theory. In

45

this sense the more basic can be said to offer us an explanation of the regularities holding in the less. It is clear that the kinetic theory has this status *vis-à-vis* the Boyle-Charles law.

In our case, the mechanistic theory would be the more basic, since it would supposedly be founded on the principles of physics and chemistry, which have an application to a much wider range of phenomena than just living beings; and it is expected that it would allow for a much finer prediction and control of human behaviour, and hence would fill in the many gaps and uncertainties in our ordinary explanations-by-motive and in those theories which have developed with these as a starting point. In other words it would prove its broader scope by allowing us to derive new, unsuspected explanations on the ordinary level of motive. This kind of performance is, of course, another of the prerogatives of a more basic theory (and has analogues with the kinetic theory above).

Thus our mechanistic theory would have to be coordinated in such a way that we could connect many of the state-descriptions in everyday language with state-descriptions cast in the language of the theory: such and such a pattern of excitation corresponds to the state of desiring peanuts, such and such another to that of feeling guilty over failing one's exams, etc. And these connections would allow us to derive plausible motive explanations from those of the theory in a large number of cases (of course, not in all: the advantage of such a mechanistic theory would presumably be that it would give us the first foolproof counter to self-deception, repression, etc., and, hence, allow for new discovery in human psychology).

Now the fact that the mechanistic theory would be a potential rival to our ordinary account has been the ground for arguments to the effect that mechanism is in some sense inconceivable. These repose on the preposterousness of the claim that our ordinary talk is radically mistaken. Malcolm's recent article seems to take a variant of this line, although here the preposterousness comes out in a kind of pragmatic paradox involved in the statement of the mechanist position.[5] But in order to make his argument stick, Malcolm is forced to show that the mechanistic account cannot be related to our ordinary one as more to less basic explanation. And it would follow from the above that any argument to the effect that mechanism is inconceivable must do the same; for if both accounts are systematically related, then there is no clash, and mechanism is freed of the embarrassing claim that our everyday consciousness of action is radically in error.

Now I believe that all arguments against the conceivability of mechanism fail because they cannot rule out this possibility of systematic coordination. Let us look at Malcolm's argument. This runs roughly as follows: If we want to set up the two kinds of explanation in canonical form, where a general proposition and a particular proposition of fact allow us to derive the *explicandum*, then there is a significant difference in logic between the two general propositions. For ordinary explanation is in terms of an inclination of the agent, as we have seen; but this means that to set it up like other explanations is to produce a major which is non-contingent. Thus supposing we explain A's doing B by saying that A saw that B leads to G. In ordinary life, we understand as given that A has goal G, and this is then a satisfactory explanation. But supposing we are asked to spell out the explanation? If we follow the model of explanation of inanimate things, we might look again at the following example: Why was there an explosion? Because A lit a match near the leaking main. In order to fill this out we need to add: and lighting matches near leaking mains produces explosions (or some general proposition from which this could be deduced with a few simple statements of fact). Now if we return to our action example, we find that what corresponds to the particular circumstances related in 'A lit a match near the leaking main' is 'A has G as a goal' and 'A sees that B leads to G'. What then takes the place of the general law about fire, gas and explosions is 'when A has goal G and sees that B leads to G, he does B'.

But translated out of this gobbledy-gook, and joined with a *ceteris paribus* clause, this is not a contingent proposition; for if A wants G and sees that he can get it by B, then if there are no deterrents or obstacles (this latter protasis being the burden of the *ceteris paribus* clause), he does B of necessity: that is, this is what we mean by 'want', for it ascribes a bent of the agent toward a certain consummation, and if with no obstacles or deterrents he fails to move in this direction, we cannot go on ascribing it to him.

But no comparable *ceteris paribus* clause will transform the major about fire, gas and explosions into a non-contingent proposition. And the difference is once more this pervasive one noted above: that our ordinary explanations are teleological, that they operate with the notion of inclination. But since the antecedent circumstances which one marshals to explain action include inclinations, the sum of these circumstances is already non-contingently likened to the *explicandum*; or to put it another way, the sum of them must show the disposition to the *explicandum*. But this means that it is not a contingent matter that *ceteris paribus* these circumstances lead to the action to be explained. The addition of a general truth proposition is therefore unnecessary, and any we do add will not be contingent.

Now Malcolm argues that since the general 'laws' of ordinary explanation are not contingent they cannot be seen as related to mechanistic laws on a more basic level; for this would mean, as we have seen, that they would be 'explained' by the latter in the sense that we would be able to express in the terms of the mechanistic theory the conditions of their holding. But, Malcolm argues, 'the a priori connection between intention or purpose and behaviour cannot fail to hold', and thus 'it cannot be contingently dependent on any contingent regularity'.[6]

But this argument is invalid; and Malcolm gives the wherewithal to answer it on the very next page. And so he must; for he wants to go on to argue that 'the verification of a comprehensible neurophysiological theory of behaviour' would refute our purposive explanations,[7] which is of course essential to his argument about the conceivability of mechanism. But if we construe these explanations as reposing on a priori principles, how can they be refuted? Malcolm is thus forced to introduce the following distinction: what cannot be shown false to all eternity is the truth that if A wants G and sees that B leads to G, then *ceteris paribus* he will do B.[8] For this depends on the meaning of 'want'. But what can be established empirically is whether or not this set of concepts, and the accompanying 'laws', really apply to human behaviour. This is enough for Malcolm's purposes, for the claim that they do not, while logically sound, is preposterous.

But if we take this distinction back to the preceding page, then the argument against more basic mechanistic explanations disappears. For we would not be claiming to show in neuro-physiology the conditions of the truth of these *a priori* proposi-tions about 'want', but only the conditions of their application to the animate organisms to which we apply them. And this seems a just statement of what such a mechanistic theory could claim to show. The logic of the two languages is very different. But this by itself is never an obstacle to the reduction of one theory to another; indeed, there is always such a non-congruence of the conceptual mesh. There would thus be nothing in the neurophysiological theory like the concept 'want', but this would not prevent us from using connecting propositions such as 'the state P_x is the state of the CNS which corresponds to what we call "wanting peanuts".' We could indeed never show why wanting peanuts is followed by trying to get peanuts, but we could show why this behaviour follows P_x; and this con-tingent nomological regularity would be what underlies (all unknown to us at present) our present use of the concept 'wanting peanuts'. The regularity makes a concept with this logic applicable, and included in the logic are 'laws' of the type Malcolm cites.

Hence, if the above reasoning is right, there is no blanket argument to the inconceivability of mechanism; we cannot argue, that is, from the fact that mechanistic explanations are irreducibly different in logic to the (teleological and intentional) explanations of ordinary life to the conclusion that a mechanistic account is untenable. But there does emerge from the above an important restriction on mechanistic explanations of behaviour: any acceptable such account must in fact be coordinated with our everyday account so as to 'save the phenomena'.

I would like now to look more closely at what this restriction involves. It does not mean, as I said above, that all the explana-tions which we accept in everyday life as valid or even obvious must be upheld by being shown to be derivable from true state-ments of the mechanistic theory. On the contrary, we would expect that many of the ideas of our present conventional wisdom would be upset. But it does mean that the type of explanation which is shown to be so derivable must be such that it upholds in the general case the logic of our ordinary language of feeling, action and desire.

An example may make clearer what is meant here. Let us say

that I am racked with guilt because I have slain my brother. Now the logic of this notion of guilt over fratricide is that the feeling is related to the thought (in this case, memory) of my killing my brother and also to a complex of other thoughts and feelings whose upshot is to present this act as a heinous offence. Now to say that the feeling according to its concept is related to these thoughts is to say something about its aetiology. Had I not killed my brother, or could I suppress the (even unconscious) memory of this act, or could I really come (in the depths of emotion and not just by a superficial judgment) to feel that it was not a terrible wrong, my guilt would be assuaged. If this aetiology is not true, that is, if one of these conditions is met and the feeling remains, then the original ascription was wrong: perhaps I am feeling guilty over something else; perhaps what I feel is not guilt at all.

Now imagine that we are accounting for this in our mechanistic theory. Then the requirement of compatibility means that our mechanistic account must back up the aetiology which is implicit in the logic of the concept used. Now the corresponding state-descriptions of the mechanistic theory will, of course, have nothing of the logic of our everyday feeling language. Corresponding to the guilt-feeling will be, say, a neurochemical state of the organism G; this in turn will be explained by, let us say, various patterns of excitation in the brain, P_1, P_2, P_3, . . . P_n. The links between these will then be purely contingent.

But the question is whether the mechanistic account supports the aetiology, and this is a question of the counterfactual and subjunctive conditionals it contains. For in general, as we have seen, two causal theories which seem to apply equally well to a given case will still be judged incompatible if the conditionals they support diverge. To say that they are coordinated is to say that they are linked in such a way that their conditionals cannot diverge.

Granted, then, that we can link the necessary conditions above, that I have killed my brother, that I remember this act, etc., with some members of the series of P-states, P_1 . . . P_n, or with the causes of P-states, the question is whether we can derive the same conditionals from the mechanistic theory together with those connecting propositions. If not, and if we accept the mechanistic theory as true, then we will have shown that the ascription of guilt over fratricide was untrue. If, for instance, we could show that the P-states linked with the memory (even unconsciously) of my killing my brother, or those linked with my seeing fractricide as wrong, had nothing to do with the feeling, and that their suppression would leave the feeling intact, then we could not go on describing this feeling as guilt about the act.

Now it is conceivable in this case that we might discover that I was self-deceived, that I was not really guilty over fratricide, but over something else; it is even conceivable that we might discover that my psychic pain was to be understood in the light of quite another feeling than guilt. We might thus find in this case that the appropriate aetiology was not backed up.

But the general requirement of compatibility is that this must be the exceptional case, rather than the rule. For if it happened in every case, this would mean that the concept 'guilt' would never be correctly applied. And that is just too much to swallow. And even if we could open our dialectical throats wide enough to swallow this, we certainly could not cope with the whole range of similar concepts which describe our feelings and aspirations: gratitude, indignation, compassion, shame, pride, remorse, awe, contempt, regret, ambition, and so on, and with the whole range of action concepts, which would have to go down if we allowed for general incompatibility between the mechanistic explanation and our ordinary language.

This problem of compatibility would arise not only where we already feel we know the explanation, as in the case above (for nothing could be clearer according to our accepted background than feeling guilt because one has killed one's brother). It is just as germane where we are still looking for an explanation. Let us suppose that an immigrant who has become very rich in the new world feels guilt about having left his native land and family. Let us say that in terms of his values, there is something irrational about this. So we look for an explanation.

Now this explanation will involve our tracing irrational leaps in unconscious thought. Perhaps an infantile sense of wrong for having acted in a certain way toward his brother extends to the thought that here he is rich today while the same brother moulders away in the native village. Perhaps even this guilt does not come out until some other development, only irrationally

51

linked with it, brings it out: let us say that the immigrant feels quite happy until the beginning of financial adversity triggers a sense that he deserves this 'punishment' which he is now receiving.

Or perhaps, rather, this guilt object is a screen; he is really guilty because he has become rich by exploiting his workers, but finds it easier to admit to himself the sense of 'wrong' over leaving his family, a feeling which he and his friends will after all go on castigating as irrational but honourable, rather than acknowledging the real object.

These and many other explanations are possible, as explanations of guilt (in both cases) or as explanations of guilt over this object (in the case of the first explanation). Compatibility means, in this example, not that our mechanistic account backs up an already known explanation, for there is none, but that it backs up an explanation which is in keeping with the logic of 'guilt over leaving family' or at least 'guilt'. There must, that is, be some account of it as guilt whose counterfactual or subjunctive conditionals are derivable from the mechanistic account and the connecting propositions.

This example is of interest because it shows, first, that while giving an account of a feeling as guilt does not mean that one accounts for it as rational guilt, this nevertheless does not abolish the distinction. If we are to be able to defend the use of the concept, the explanation must make the feeling understandable as one of guilt, and this involves reference to wrong or sin for which we are responsible; in short it involves reference to the 'guilty'. This may take the form of a childish sense of wrongdoing earlier experienced, which we have long ceased to judge as wrong, and hence may be irrational; and even further irrationality may enter in, such as in the case above when the guilt is triggered by the financial adversity perceived as 'punishment'. But we remain within the same circle of ideas, and must, if we are to speak of 'guilt'.

The requirement of compatibility is thus that there be some explanation based on these ideas which is supported by the mechanistic account, in the sense that its conditionals are derivable from those of the mechanistic account in the way mentioned in the previous paragraph.

And this case shows, second, that once more the principle of compatibility which we demand that mechanistic explanations fulfil has nothing necessarily to do with supporting the explanations of behaviour which we currently may accept, that it applies even where we have the wrong explanation or confess ourselves to have none at all. The principle does claim, however, to put a limit on possible types of mechanistic theory, namely, that they must provide accounts which, *via* the connecting propositions linking theoretical states with action and feeling descriptions, support explanations of our actions and feelings which do not violate the logic of the terms we use to describe them—if indeed not invariably, then at least generally and for the most part. And this on pain of saddling us with the preposterous conclusion that we have been talking nonsense all these millenia, that the criteria for the application of our ordinary terms for feeling and behaviour are never or hardly ever met.

What are the consequences for the pursuit of the sciences of behaviour which flow from this principle of compatibility? Well, first, that *a priori* arguments against a more basic mechanistic explanation, such as that cited from Malcolm above, are invalid.

But second, the idea of a science of behaviour which could link 'receptor impulse' and 'colourless movement' via some theory of the brain and CNS, and which might have no relation at all to our ordinary vocabulary and the distinctions it marks, which would give us no basis for distinctions, e.g. like that between shame and guilt, or anger and indignation, and so on, treating these in the way that post-Galilean physics treats, e.g. the Aristotelian distinction between supra- and sub-lunar—this idea is an epistemological monstrosity.

It follows, thirdly, that any mechanistic theory which can claim to account for behaviour will have to be rich enough to incorporate the basis of a very wide range of distinctions which, at present, mark the intentional world of human agents and which are essential to understand their behaviour. I have mentioned above just a few important feeling-terms which are general to men. But incorporated into the description of much of human behaviour is some reference to the set of institutions in which men live and are formed (as seen by them, either in terms of their own descriptions, or in terms of their real meaning for them), to the set of social meanings on the basis of which they operate to understand themselves and each other, and so on. And these, of course, vary greatly with the culture, or even in some cases the circle to which people belong.

Imagine that we are accounting for the following event: a vassal remains covered in the presence of the king, and this he does deliberately as an incitement to revolt, or even perhaps as a signal to his confederates to rise. Now any explanation of this event must support counterfactuals which involve reference to kingship, revolt, the symbolism of uncovering oneself before majesty, and so on. For it must be true that our hero would not have remained covered, had he not perceived this man entering the room as the king, rather than as the new pretender whom he supports. And that he would not have remained covered, either if this act had not had this significance of refusing allegiance or if his forces had not been ready (in the case where this is a signal to rise), and so on. Unless these counterfactuals or others like them are true, our original description is in jeopardy.

Central to any understanding of human behaviour which starts from explanation by motive is the fact that man is a cultural animal, that his behaviour can vary very widely, and that these variations must be understood in the light of the differences in human culture. This is not to say that explanation must always be couched in the language of the given culture, but a people's self-understanding must be among the things which any adequate theory can explain. We must therefore be able to express in our theory the major distinctions by which men understand the differences in their behaviour from person to person and time to time. And this means that a neurophysiological mechanist theory must have this property as well.

It follows from this that the idea of such a mechanistic science as representing a simpler road than a science of behaviour which comes to grips with human culture is an illusion. Our neurophysiological theory will have to be rich enough to mark the major distinctions of all the varied human cultures. We can only explain behaviour in terms of what goes on 'under-the-skin' if we incorporate 'under-the-skin' state-descriptions corresponding to all the wide range of furniture of the human agent's intentional environment, the inventory of which requires that one explore the entire range of his culture. For a neurophysiological short-cut which by-passed cultural differences would make nonsense of a great part of the descriptions men use to speak of themselves.

Hence the requirement to 'save the phenomena' defines a criterion that any neurophysiological theory must meet to be worth considering. Of course, this criterion can and should be developed in greater detail, and in some dimensions with considerable exactness. Recent developments in psycho-linguistics provide a good example. Unless we want to by-pass altogether the distinction between understanding and not understanding a sentence, or finding it well- or ill-formed, which would once more be preposterous, our explanation of verbal behaviour has to be able to account for the full complexity of the operations by which we form and recognize these sentences. Any approach which does not address itself to this requirement is not worth pursuing.

In the foregoing we have considered some arguments which could serve as the antithesis to mechanism in our antinomy. As blanket arguments against the conceivability of mechanism, they cannot be sustained; but something interesting does necessarily come out of all this, *viz.* a restriction on any mechanistic theory, that it must 'save the phenomena' by generating the distinctions which underlie our vocabulary of action and feeling and those implicit in our culture. Now this may suggest to us that after all the sharp opposition between neurophysiological explanation and our ordinary account might be misguided.

What if, in order to generate the rich variety of distinctions which must be saved, future neurophysiological theory found it necessary to enrich its vocabulary and hence its conceptual armoury? And supposing that the new ranges of concepts incorporated some of the purposive and intentional force of our current ordinary vocabulary? This would be the case, for instance, if certain global patterns of excitation in the brain and nervous system could be adequately understood in their functioning, conditions and consequences only if we identified them partly in terms of or in relation to the psychological processes or states they mediate.

It is very difficult to say anything very sensible about this prospective conceptual enrichment at this stage, just because any conceptual innovation cannot be mapped until it has occurred. All I can claim at this stage is that we have no reason to look on our present categories as so fixed that a conceptual convergence of this form is ruled out. It is therefore perfectly conceivable that we may move toward a neurophysiological theory which will not be reductive, in the sense that it will not show teleological and intentional concepts to be eliminable at a more basic level. If this were to be the case, then the problems connected with the above antinomy would disappear.

This statement of possibility is all that can be argued at this stage, as I said above. But it is evident that even this will not be accepted without argument; and so I must turn now to the other side of the antinomy, the arguments in favour of the thesis of mechanism. It seems to me that these fall basically into two categories, the methodological and the ontological.

The crux of the methodological argument is the belief mentioned above that any explanation other than a mechanistic one leaves some questions unanswered. If we introduce purposive concepts, like the famous 'entelechies' of vitalism, then we simply close off certain questions, *viz.* those dealing with the mechanisms which underlie the functions specified by our entelechies. This would only be justifiable if there were nothing here to discover, but the history of biology rather leads us to believe the opposite. Great progress has been made by attempting to discover the mechanisms underlying certain holistic functions; we have only to think of the recent breakthrough by Crick and others which has opened the mechanisms of cell-replication.

Now this is less an argument from logical necessity than it is a persuasive use of historical analogy.[9] Even if in the past the introduction of non-mechanist concepts has closed avenues which turned out to be worth exploring, this does nothing to show that such consequences necessarily follow on the use of such concepts. But the case for the possibility of convergence can be presented in a more positive light. The kind of conceptual enrichment alluded to above would not necessarily have the effect of closing off further enquiry concerning the phenomena characterized, as has been widely claimed for Driesch's entelechies; on the contrary, we can imagine a whole range of questions which would open on the border of psychology and neurophysiology. Others, including some avenues of enquiry of a strictly mechanist kind, would be closed. But it is true of any range of explanatory concepts that in characterizing a given range of reality by means of them we open some avenues of enquiry and close others. Nothing can be concluded from this in general about the validity of any given range; it all depends how fruitful are the avenues opened and closed. And this we can only find out by looking; no *a priori* arguments are valid.

Hence arguments from striking historical parallels, like vitalism, cannot be conclusive *a priori*. For they all depend on clinching the case that the parallel really holds, and this may depend on our showing that in practice the new range of concepts has the same drawbacks as others putatively similar have had. Thus a fault of vitalism is that it seemed to allow no place at all for further enquiry, but this cannot be claimed about future conceptual enrichment of the type I am suggesting until we have a chance to examine actual cases of suggested conceptual revisions and additions.

The fact is that many of the great paradigms of scientific progress can be used to teach more than one lesson. Does the revolution in physics in the seventeenth century tell in favour of mechanism because it was mechanist, or does it show rather how the hold of a powerful traditional conceptual scheme (Aristotelian in the seventeenth century; mechanist, in ours) on the scientific community can impede progress? We shall have to await the outcome of present disputes to see who has been cast in the role of Galileo and who in that of his obtuse Aristotelian critics.

The ontological objection is deeper and harder to state and, hence, naturally, to criticize. But it goes something like this: human beings are after all physical objects; they must therefore obey the laws of physics and chemistry, those which have been found true for all physical objects. It follows that some form of reductivism must hold, that is, that higher level explanations, like the psychological, the sociological, etc., must be ultimately explicable on a more basic level, in terms of physics and chemistry; on the way down this reductivist road, we would obviously pass a neurophysiological stage.

In order to see the necessity of reductionism here, the argument runs, we have to examine the alternatives. If there were true explanations of behaviour on the psychological level which were not reducible to a neurophysiological account (as a first step, of course, but all the questions of principle can be posed about this first step) and hence were not coordinated with this more basic explanation, then it follows (as we saw above) either that one or other of these accounts must be inadequate in some respect, or else that they hold of different things. Since by hypothesis the psychological account is valid, we have to conclude either that the neurophysiological account is inadequate, that is, that on its own it goes astray at certain points (the points of conflict), or else that the psychological account applies to something which the neurophysiological account cannot encompass. But the latter conclusion amounts to some form or other of mind-body dualism, for it entails that there is a level of reality accessible to psychological description and explanation, description of which cannot be formulated in neurophysiological terms. Or else this level of reality would provide a set of events susceptible of neurophysiological explanation, and this would land us back in the first alternative.

Now this first alternative is unacceptable, because it amounts to saying that the laws of neurophysiology (and hence at lower stages those of physics and chemistry) have exceptions at those points where there is conflict with our psychological explanations. But a doctrine of exceptionalism seems hard to justify intellectually. We are thus forced back on to dualism, but this scarcely seems plausible to the contemporary mind, even if *sub specie aeterni* it may be as tenable as any other hypothesis. We have trouble believing that there are functions of the mind which are not in some sense embodied in neural activity of some kind or other (though this is not the same thing as holding what is called among contemporary philosophers the 'identity theory', for this involves a prior acceptance *holus bolus* of mechanism). But quite apart from this, the form of dualism entailed by this horn of the dilemma is a particularly implausible one, since it involves non-interference between the two realms of mind and matter. For if what goes on on the psychological level were to have an effect on the neurophysiological level, then there would be some interruption in the smooth operation of neurophysiological function according to neurophysiological laws; and once more these laws would have exceptions.

But how could we even exist as rational life if the realms of mind and matter functioned independently of each other? Hence they must be coordinated. But how coordinated if not by systematic relation between the causal laws? The only alternative model of coordination would seem to be some rather fantastic hypothesis like Malebranchian occasionalism. The weirdness of such occasionalist hypotheses may force the dualist back into the notion that mind and body after all interact; but then by this he only succeeds in impaling himself on both horns of the dilemma at once, for he holds both dualism and exceptionalism and seems to have involved himself in a set of insuperable epistemological problems.

Now since this whole dilemma arises from denying that there is a systematic relation between valid psychological explanations and those on a lower level, we seem bound to accept this premise. But if we accept systematic relation, then there can be little doubt that the neurophysiological (and later the physicochemical) is the more basic level; for these laws apply to a wider range of phenomena, and the 'higher' explanations must represent special cases of these. Lower must mean more basic here, and everything must be reducible to physics and chemistry.

Something like this underlies the current faith in mechanism. The argument is powerful as long as we remain with the old fixed alternatives; but once we examine a hypothesis like that of conceptual convergence above, its weaknesses come to light. In fact, there are two related places where key questions are begged. One is hidden in expressions like 'the laws of physics and chemistry' or 'the laws of neurophysiology'; the other is hidden in the terms 'governed by' or 'apply' when used in connection with these laws.

To take the first one: on the convergence hypothesis I adumbrated above, it will be true that all behaviour will be accounted for in neurophysiological terms, only the neurophysiological theory adequate to this purpose will be an enriched one relative to what we know at present. When we put it in this way, the mechanistic argument founders; for it amounts to a denial *a priori* that such an enrichment will prove necessary or possible; and who can justify this? It would have been as absurd for nineteenth-century mechanist physics to have denied that any conceptual enrichment would be necessary in order to account for physical phenomena. Some physicists were tempted then, but no one would make such a denial on behalf of contemporary physics.

The mechanist argument rests here on an equivocation on 'the laws of neurophysiology'. If one wishes to avoid dualism and all its consequences, one will hold that in some sense we can give a neurophysiological account of all behaviour, for all behaviour has a neurophysiological embodiment and, so, falls *ipso facto* into its domain. But the sense of 'neurophysiological account' which figures in this denial of dualism is not restricted as to the explanatory concepts deployed; the term here means only an explanation which accounts for neurophysiological phenomena. The equivocation lies between this quite general sense and one which is closer to 'account in terms of the presently accepted concepts of neurophysiology and extensions of them'. By moving from one to the other unconsciously, we can believe that we have ruled out the kind of conceptual convergence I mentioned above by the argument against dualism. Indeed, one *can believe* that the only alternatives are dualism and the present assumptions of the science. And this is really the crucial belief; if one accepts this, then it is easy to identify all neurophysiological explanation with explanations according to present canons. But this premise is far from necessary.

This equivocation on 'the laws of . . .' (neurophysiology or physics or chemistry) also underpins the view that our hypothesis of convergence is exceptionalist or interactionist. For it lies behind the whole dilemma which forces us into some such position to avoid dualism, by defining any novel explanatory principles as outside 'the laws of neurophysiology' (or physics or chemistry). But the accusation of interactionism is backed up by another equivocation, that on notions like 'governed by' (laws), or (laws) 'applying'. This may still worry us even when we have set aside as an unimportant verbal question how we are going to use expressions like 'the laws of physics' or 'the laws of neurophysiology'.

The worry can perhaps be expressed most clearly in connection with physico-chemical explanation. If the principles of such explanations as we know them now are not adequate to account for the behaviour of animate beings, or of men, while remaining generally appropriate for the rest of nature, then surely there must be something very odd about animate beings. For those laws of physics and chemistry which apply to nature in general will somehow not apply, or will at least admit of exceptions, in the case of animals; and is this idea not a species of exceptionalism—once we admit, that is, that animate beings are also physical beings *à part entière*—that is, once we abandon any form of dualism? It must follow, therefore, that animate behaviour must be explicable in terms of the laws of physics and chemistry and, hence, that all other explanations must be reducible to those in terms of these laws, where 'the laws of physics and chemistry' designates simply those laws which are found to apply to the whole domain of nature, whatever these turn out to be. The argument hence avoids *a priori* legislation concerning these laws.

Now, of course, the argument in these terms does not necessarily rule out non-mechanist explanations of behaviour, if we accept as possible some Teilhardian hypothesis in which we might need enriched concepts to deal adequately with inanimate nature as well. But even leaving aside such long shots, the argument does not hold. There is no reason in general to hold that animate behaviour must be accountable for by the same principles as inanimate—outside of the notion that since animate behaviour is, like everything else in nature, governed by the general laws of physics and chemistry, it cannot also be governed by other principles, without these in some sense breaching these general laws and, hence, creating exceptions.

But this notion is based on a confusion which centres in the notion of 'governed by'.[10] Thus to say that a range of things is governed by a certain set of laws, defining, say, a given force, is not to say that these laws can account for all the behaviour of things of this range; we may have to invoke laws defining some other force to explain what occurs. Moreover both forces may operate on the same behaviour, so that we have to invoke both together to explain certain events. Such is the case with gravity and electromagnetism, for instance, in physics. To put it crudely, one can lift things with a magnet that otherwise would fall to or remain on the ground.

But in these cases, even if we might speak of one force 'interfering' with the other, in that if one were to cease operating, the course of events determined uniquely by the other would be different from what it in fact is, it would still be absurd, for example, were we to start with a physics which recognized only gravity and then modify it to take account of magnetism, for us to say that we had discovered that not all bodies are 'governed by' the law of gravity after all. That is not what we mean by 'governed by'; rather gravity remains essential to our understanding how things behave even when we discover with the operation of other forces that things are more complicated. The fact that things would be different if, in some way rather difficult to imagine, gravity were the only force operating on bodies is neither here nor there, unless anthropomorphically we want to think of gravity as taking umbrage at this.

A similar reasoning applies to our problem. On my convergence hypothesis above, the present principles of neurophysiology, and *a fortiori* those of physics and chemistry, would be supplemented by concepts of quite a different kind, in which, for instance, relations of meaning might become relevant to neurophysiological process. If this turned out to be of explanatory value, then, we could conclude that these new principles also govern the phenomena. We can hope that the predictions we make with the aid of these new explanatory concepts differ from these which would be made with an exclusive reliance on the old ones, for otherwise there would have been little point in introducing them. In this sense, the new 'forces' can be said to 'interfere'. But it would be absurd to say that our hypothesis entails that the original principles no longer govern the phenomena, that we have found 'exceptions' to them.

In fact we would only be tempted to say that a given range of laws suffered exceptions if the additional 'forces' could not be understood in terms of *any* principles, but remained quite refractory to scientific explanation of any kind. What underlies this accusation of exceptionalism is, in fact, the deep-seated prejudice that scientific explanation is impossible on other than mechanistic principles. If we accept this premise, then we can reason that any attempt to supplement our existing scientific languages with non-mechanist principles can only introduce gaps in our explanations, and to believe that this is justified one would have to hold to some kind of exceptionalism.

The argument which flows from the confusion around the term 'governed by', like that around the term 'the laws of . . .' which we discussed above, thus reposes in the end on the identification of scientific laws and explanation in general with laws and explanations based on principles currently in vogue, *viz.* mechanistic ones. It is only by accepting this identification that we can show that the only alternatives to reductionism are dualism and exceptionalism. But then the reductive argument against our convergence hypothesis, which aims to prove that non-mechanistic explanation of this kind won't do, assumes what it sets out to prove. It can only get going if we assume mechanism from the start.

In other words, to look on a conceptual enrichment of neurophysiology of the kind I have been discussing as a species of exceptionalism, as a claim that the laws of neurophysiology and a portion of physics and chemistry don't apply, is to have covertly identified the laws of science *tout court* with laws of the type now in vogue. If this were the case, then indeed, the introduction of any other principle of explanation would be tantamount to a claim that these laws don't apply universally, don't govern all the phenomena. And thus we could argue that all higher level explanations must be reducible to physico-chemical ones, else they cannot be considered scientific explanations.

But if we define mechanistic explanation as we did at the beginning, as a form of explanation which eschews teleological and intentional concepts, and mechanism as the doctrine that all scientific explanation must be of this type, then we have in this identification a mechanist premise. And this means that the reductive argument against our convergence hypothesis, which is an alternative to mechanism, is based on a *petitio principii*; it can only get going if we assume that mechanism is right from the start.

The arguments for this side of the antinomy, the thesis of mechanism, have not fared any better than those for the other side. In fact, mechanism is neither a certainty, as the sole metaphysic compatible with science, as its protagonists claim, nor is it inconceivable, and necessarily doomed to deny the undeniable, as some philosophers have argued. But in examining these invalid arguments, some clarity has been gained. What this examination seems to point toward is a dissolution of the alternative mechanism-dualism; it invites us to examine a nondualistic conception of man which is nevertheless not linked with a reductivist notion of the sciences of man. This would, of course, involve an ontology with more than one level; in other words, it would mean that although some principles govern the behaviour of all things, others apply only to some; and yet the latter cannot be shown as special cases of the former.

This hypothesis flies in the face of entrenched dogmas of our scientific tradition. But I believe it has the merit of plausibility when we come to the sciences of man. And it would have the incidental benefit of surmounting the antinomy of mechanism.

NOTE: An earlier version of this paper, delivered at the Loyota University Centennial Celebration, October 1970, has been published in A. Karazmar and J. C. Eccles, *Brain and Human Behavior*, Springer-Verlag, 1970.

REFERENCES

[1] *Cf.* M. Grene, 'Reducibility—Another Side Issue?' in this volume, pp. 14–37.
[2] G. Ryle, *Dilemmas*: Cambridge University Press, 1954.
[3] A. I. Melden, *Free Action*, London: Routledge & Kegan Paul, 1961.
[4] E. Nagel, *The Structure of Science*, New York: Harcourt, Brace & World, 1961, pp. 353–4, 433–5.
[5] N. Malcolm, 'The Conceivability of Mechanism' in *Philosophical Review*, 77, 1968, pp. 45–72.
[6] *Ibid.*, p. 50.
[7] *Ibid.*, p. 51.
[8] *Loc. cit.*
[9] See footnote 1 above.
[10] *Ibid.*

4

THE HOMUNCULUS FALLACY

Anthony J. P. Kenny

We are persons, and the resistance to reductivism springs often, perhaps chiefly, from our resistance to the mockery we must make of ourselves in its terms. One error we should guard against, Dr Kenny argues, is to read the operations of parts of persons or of their bodies as exactly equivalent to those of persons themselves. His paper is based on remarks made by him at our conference on 'Concepts of Mind', in response to the arguments presented during the course of the meeting by the participants from psychology and neurology, especially by Professor Richard Gregory, to whose published statements he refers in the text. Dr Kenny's argument, though not inconsistent with the previous papers, goes farther than they in its opposition to reductivistic explanation: it shows us emphatically where we may take a stand in working toward a new—or perhaps renewed—philosophical synthesis. Professor Rorty's reply points up the difficulty, for philosophers in the mainstream of current academic debate and analysis, of accepting his thesis, especially in relation to received views of scientific explanation, and Kenny's reply further consolidates his previous argument.

In the *Philosophical Investigations*, Wittgenstein says: 'Only of a human being and what resembles (behaves like) a living human being can one say: it has sensations; it sees; is blind; hears; is deaf; is conscious or unconscious.'[1] This dictum is often rejected in practice by psychologists, physiologists and computer experts, when they take predicates whose normal application is to complete human beings or complete animals and apply them to parts of animals, such as brains, or to electrical systems. This is commonly defended as a harmless pedagogical device; I wish to argue that it is a dangerous practice which may lead to conceptual and methodological confusion. I shall call the reckless application of human-being predicates to insufficiently human-like objects the 'homunculus fallacy', since its most naïve form

65

is tantamount to the postulation of a little man within a man to explain human experience and behaviour.

One of the first philosophers to draw attention to the homunculus fallacy was Descartes. In his *Dioptrics*, he describes how 'the objects we look at produce very perfect images in the back of the eyes.'[2] He encourages his readers to convince themselves of this by taking the eye of a newly dead man, replacing with paper or eggshell the enveloping membranes at the back, and placing it inside a shutter so as to let light through it into an otherwise dark room. 'You will see (I dare say with surprise and pleasure) a picture representing in natural perspective all the objects outside.' 'You cannot doubt' he continues 'that a quite similar picture is produced in a living man's eye, on the lining membrane . . . Further, the images are not only produced in the back of the eye but also sent on to the brain . . . and when it is thus transmitted to the inside of our head, the picture still retains some degree of its resemblance to the objects from which it originates.' But he concludes with a warning. 'We must not think that it is by means of this resemblance that the picture makes us aware of the objects—as though we had another pair of eyes to see it, inside our brain.'[3]

To think of the brain as having eyes and seeing the retinal image would be one way of committing the homunculus fallacy. But in spite of warning us against the fallacy at this point, Descartes himself commits it when he comes to discuss the relationship between the soul and the pineal gland:

> If we see some animal approach us, the light reflected from its body depicts two images of it, one in each of our eyes, and these two images form two others, by means of the optic nerves, in the interior surface of the brain which faces its cavities; then from there, by means of the animal spirits with which its cavities are filled, these images so radiate towards the little gland which is surrounded by these spirits, that the movement which forms each point of one of the images tends towards the same point of the gland towards which tends the movement which forms the point of the other image which represents the same part of this animal. By this means the two images which are in the brain form but one upon the gland, which, acting

immediately upon the soul, causes it to see the form of this animal.[4]

To speak of the soul encountering images in the pineal gland is to commit the homunculus fallacy; for *pace* Descartes, a soul is no more a complete human being than a brain is. In itself, there is nothing philosophically incorrect in speaking of images in the brain: Descartes himself is anxious to explain that they are very schematic images and not pictures except in a metaphorical sense:

No images have to resemble the objects they represent in all respects . . . resemblance in a few features is enough, and very often the perfection of an image depends on its not resembling the object as much as it might. For instance, engravings, which consist merely of a little ink spread over paper, represent to us forests, towns, men and even battles and tempests.[5]

There would be nothing philosophically objectionable in the suggestion that these schematic images might be observed by a brain surgeon investigating the gland. What is misleading is the suggestion that these images are visible to the *soul*, whose perception of them constitutes seeing. What is wrong is that exactly the same sorts of problems arise about Descartes' explanation as about his *explicandum*. To the Aristotelians who preceded Descartes, seeing necessitated a non-mechanistic phenomenon taking place in the eye. Descartes introduced new mechanisms, but in his system the non-mechanistic event in the eye is replaced by a new non-mechanistic reading of patterns in the pineal gland. The interaction between mind and matter is philosophically as puzzling a few inches behind the eye as it is in the eye itself.

One danger, then, of the homunculus fallacy is that in problems concerning perception and kindred matters it conceals what is left to be explained. In the case of Descartes, we are put on our guard by the quaintness of some of the physiology, so that we have no difficulty in discovering the gaps in his account; but the philosophical hiatus can coexist with much more sophisticated physiological information.

A contemporary expert on perception, Professor R. L.

Gregory, at the beginning of his book *The Eye and the Brain*, echoes Descartes' warning against the homunculus fallacy:

> We are so familiar with seeing, that it takes a leap of imagination to realise that there are problems to be solved. But consider it. We are given tiny distorted upside-down images in the eyes, and we see separate solid objects in surrounding space. From the patterns of stimulation on the retinas we perceive the world of objects, and this is nothing short of a miracle.
>
> The eye is often described as like a camera, but it is the quite uncamera-like features of perception which are most interesting. How is information from the eyes coded into neural terms, into the language of the brain, and reconstituted into experience of surrounding objects? The task of eye and brain is quite different from either a photographic or a television camera converting objects merely into images. There is a temptation, which must be avoided, to say that the eyes produce pictures in the brain. A picture in the brain suggests the need of some kind of internal eye to see it but this would need a further eye to see *its* picture . . . and so on in an endless regress of eyes and pictures. This is absurd. What the eyes do is to feed the brain with information coded into neural activity—chains of electrical impulses—which by their code and the patterns of brain activity, represent objects. We may take an analogy from written language: the letters and words on this page have certain meanings, to those who know the language. They affect the reader's brain appropriately, but they are not pictures. When we look at something, the pattern of neural activity represents the object and to the brain *is* the object. No internal picture is involved.[6]

The warning against the fallacy is excellent; but the fallacy is itself implied in the suggestion that the brain knows a language and that it has an object like the objects of perception. A converse fallacy is committed when it is said that we are given tiny, distorted, upside-down images in the eyes and that we perceive patterns of stimulation on the retina. Here it is not a bogus subject of perception which is being supplied, but a bogus object of perception.

68

The reader may feel that this is completely unfair criticism. The words I have criticized are taken from the first page of a popular book. What is the harm in personifying parts of the body in order to dramatize scientific information which can be stated in completely neutral metaphor-free language? Whether dramatization is good pedagogy depends on whether the important events happen on or off stage. The overall psychological problem of perception could be stated as follows: how does a human being cope with the available sensory information, and how does he act on it? Or, in one of Gregory's own formulations, how does information control behaviour? Now this is a problem which would still remain to be solved even if we knew every detail of the process of collection and storage of information; and one crucial aspect of it is the same whether the information is in the world, in the retinas, or in the CNS. The problem is this: what is the relation between the presence of information in the technical sense of communication theory and the possession of information in the non-technical sense in which one can acquire information about the world by looking?

For if having information is the same as knowing, then containing information is not the same as having information. An airline schedule contains the information about airline departures; but the airline schedule does not *know* the time of departures of the flights. The illiterate slave on whose shaven scalp the tyrant has tattooed his state secrets does not *know* the information which his head contains.

A category difference is involved here. To contain information is to be in a certain state, while to know something is to possess a certain capacity. A state (such as being a certain shape or size, or having a certain multiplicity or mathematical structure) is something describable by its internal properties; a capacity (such as the ability to run a four minute mile or to speak French) is describable only by specification of what would count as the exercise of the capacity. States and capacities are of course connected: in the simplest case there is an obvious connection between being a round peg (state) and being able to fit into a round hole (capacity). But the connections are not always (as in that case) analytic; and many forms of expertise consist in knowing which states go with which capacities (e.g. what types

69

of mushroom are poisonous, which alloys will stand which strains).

Knowledge is not a state but a capacity, and a capacity of a unique kind. The state of containing certain information is no doubt connected with the capacity which is knowledge of a certain fact; but the two are not identical as the earlier examples show. We may wonder what extra is involved in the knowing that p over and above containing the information that p. What is knowing a capacity to do, and what counts as an exercise of that capacity? Clearly, there is no simple answer. One cannot specify behaviour typical of knowing as one can specify behaviour typical of anger. One cannot even specify behaviour typical of knowing that p, for a given p; what behaviour the knowledge that p will lead to will depend on what one wants. For instance, knowledge that the window is open will lead to different behaviour in the case of someone who wants it open and in the case of someone who wants it shut. To be sure, the verbal utterance of 'p' is an activity which is uniquely expressive of the knowledge or belief that p; but even so, this does not at all mean that anyone who knows that p will ever say that p.

There is, then, no simple way of specifying how knowledge gets expressed in behaviour and why some pieces of knowledge do not seem to affect one's behaviour at all. Still, to know is to have the ability to modify one's behaviour in indefinite ways relevant to the pursuit of one's goals. It is because the airline schedule does not have any behaviour to be modified by what is written on it that it does not know what the flight times are.

Let us return from knowing to seeing. Seeing, when not illusory, involves knowing: vision might be defined, crudely, circularly, but not uninformatively, as the acquisition of knowledge in the visual mode. In the Aristotelian tradition, prior to Descartes, it used to be said that it was not the eye that saw, nor the soul, but the whole organism. This was because the normal way to discover whether an organism sees is not just to study its eyes, but to investigate whether its behaviour is affected by changes of light and colour, etc. Consequently, an explanation of seeing must be an explanation not only of the acquisition and storage of information, but also of what makes the containing of this information into knowledge—i.e. its relation to behaviour.

70

In his paper 'On How So Little Information Controls So Much Behaviour', Gregory well says:

> Perhaps the most fundamental question in the whole field of experimental psychology is: how far is behaviour controlled by currently available sensory information, and how far by information already stored in the central nervous system?[7]

But in that paper he presents a theory of seeing as selection of internal models without saying how the internal models are related to behaviour. He speaks of a model 'calling up the appropriate muscle power',[8] for lifting a certain weight, and of models 'mediating appropriate behaviour',[9] but he nowhere shows how these metaphors might be turned into literal language. What he really explains is how information of a certain type might reach the brain. Now let us suppose that his explanation of this proves completely correct. Even so, the crucial problem remains; and what is still to be done is masked for the reader, if not for Gregory himself, by the use of homunculus predicates of the brain and the use of intentional or representational or symbolic predicates of items in the brain. Consider the following passage from the same paper:

> In general the eye's images are biologically important only in so far as non-optical features can be read from the internal models they select. Images are merely patches of light—which cannot be eaten or be dangerous—but they serve as symbols for selecting internal models, which include the non-visual features vital to survival. It is this reading of object characteristics from images that *is* visual perception.[10]

But even if this mechanism is essential for visual perception, it is not visual perception. Selection of internal models would be possible, as seeing would not, in an isolated optical system incapable of behaviour. This is not just the ordinary language point—'we wouldn't *call* such a thing seeing'—it is a methodological point concerning the nature of the problems to be solved and the reasonableness of extrapolations from acquired results. The illusion that what is described is visual perception is encouraged by the use of language such as 'features can be *read*' and '*symbols* for selecting'.

Later in the same paper Gregory writes:

> On this general view perception is not directly of sensory information but rather of the internal models selected by sensory information. Indeed the current perception is the prevailing set of models.[11]

Clearly, it is inadequate to explain what perception is by saying that it is perception not of X but of Y: if I wonder what *perception* is, how am I helped by being told that it is of Y rather than of X? Gregory senses this: that is why his first statement of this thesis is followed by 'indeed' followed by a statement of an incompatible thesis. Perception cannot both be *of* the models and be the models.

So far my objection to the homunculus model has been that it is pedagogically and methodologically dangerous, as helping to cloak the nature of problems to be solved. But there is a more dangerous effect of the model which alone really deserves the name 'fallacy'.

Let us suppose that we waive our objections to the use of human-being predicates for non-human-beings like brains. Let us allow it to be said that the brain is P, where P is some predicate whose natural application is to whole human beings. (It may, after all, be used in quotes. It usually is—the first time.) There is still an important temptation to be resisted: the temptation to argue from

This man is P

to   This man's brain is P

or *vice versa*. Gregory does not always resist this temptation. At the beginning of the quoted paper he argues that learning or storing particular events is always ontogenetic. Naturally stored information, he says, has two origins: ancestral disasters, and previous experience of the individual stored as 'memory' (his quotes).[12] To prove that storage of particular events is always ontogenetic, he says:

> What is certain is that information gained phylogenetically is always of the general 'skill' kind. We are not able to recall individual events experienced by our ancestors.[13]

72

And *à propos* of learning skills such as tennis and piano playing, he says:

> We may be able to recall the odd particular games or concerts, but as skills it is not individual past events which are stored, but rather appropriate behaviour and strategies.[14]

Here the homunculus fallacy is committed thus: 'X remembers that p' is being treated as equivalent to 'X has stored the event that p'. The only reason given for saying that information about particular events is not stored phylogenetically is that we cannot recall individual events in our ancestors' lives. But this is to argue from 'this man is not P' to 'this man's brain is not P' which is fallacious, even if the man's brain's being P is a necessary condition for his own being P.

In another paper, 'Perceptual Illusions and Brain Models', Gregory considers whether the brain is best regarded as a digital or as an analogue device. He writes:

> It is most implausible to suppose that the brain of a child contains mathematical analyses of physical situations. When a child builds a house of toy bricks, balancing them to make walls and towers, we cannot suppose that the structural problems are solved by employing analytical mathematical techniques, involving concepts such as centre of gravity and coefficient of friction of masses. It is far better to make the lesser claim for children and animals: that they behave appropriately to objects by using analogues of senses object-properties, without involving mathematical analyses of the properties of objects and their interactions. Perceptual learning surely cannot require the learning of mathematics. It is far more plausible to suppose that it involves the building of quite simple analogues of relevant properties of objects: relevant so far as they concern the behaviour of the animal or the child.[15]

Here the homunculus fallacy is committed in the sentence, 'Perceptual learning surely cannot require the learning of mathematics'. It is the child that is doing the perceptual learning; what, if anything, is supposed to be learning mathematics is the child's brain. It is implausible that a child building toy bricks should know advanced mathematics; but from this nothing at all follows about what information is contained in the child's brain.

I conclude that there is good reason to heed the warning of Wittgenstein with which this paper began. The moral is not that the human-being predicates cannot have their use extended at all, but that they must be extended cautiously and self-consciously, and that if they are extended one may not argue from the application of such a predicate to a whole human being to the application of the transferred predicate to anything other than the whole human being.

REFERENCES

[1] L. Wittgenstein, *Philosophical Investigations* (tr. G. E. M. Anscombe): Oxford University Press, 1953, Part I, §281.
[2] R. Descartes, 'Dioptrics' in *Philosophical Writings* (trs and eds E. Anscombe and P. T. Geach), London: Nelson, 1954, pp. 239–56, 244.
[3] *Ibid.*, pp. 245–6.
[4] R. Descartes, 'Passions of the Soul', in *The Philosophical Works of Descartes*, I (trs and eds E. S. Haldane and G. R. T. Ross), pp. 329–429, 348.
[5] Descartes, in Anscombe and Geach, *loc. cit.*
[6] R. L. Gregory, *The Eye and the Brain*, New York: McGraw-Hill, 1966, p. 7.
[7] R. L. Gregory, 'On How So Little Information Controls So Much Behaviour', Bionics Research Reports, no. 1, April 1968, p. 1. This paper was also published in *Towards a Theoretical Biology* II (ed. C. H. Waddington): Edinburgh University Press, 1969, pp. 236–46.
[8] *Ibid.*, p. 8.
[9] *Loc. cit.*
[10] *Ibid.*, p. 5.
[11] *Ibid.*, p. 8.
[12] *Ibid.*, p. 1.
[13] *Loc. cit.*
[14] *Loc. cit.*
[15] R. L. Gregory, 'Perceptual Illusions and Brain Models', *Proceedings of the Royal Society B, 171*, 1968, pp. 279–96, 294.

NOT EVERY HOMUNCULUS SPOILS THE ARGUMENT

Amélie Rorty

To call a mode of argumentation or analysis a 'fallacy' is to suggest that people ought to stop using it. Any mode of analysis can be misunderstood or misapplied without itself being fallacious. It is, indeed, difficult to imagine any type of argument that does not run the risk of blocking inquiry by being misused or misdirected, though of course some arguments court more dangers than others. I do not believe that the homunculus metaphor involves a fallacy in the sense that its use exemplifies a demonstrably invalid form of argument. It can, however, mislead the unwary, and Kenny quite properly warns us against the sorts of confusions that may arise from a loose use of the metaphor.

Kenny's discussion of the 'homunculus fallacy' may be understood as a warning, or (in its stronger form) as a claim that certain arguments are fallacious. In its weaker form, his warning is that we should not mistake a metaphor for an explanation, not confuse either a mechanistic or a microstructural description of a process with the philosophical or conceptual analysis of that process, not 'reduce' the activities of persons to the states or motions of their physical parts. Properly understood, Kenny's warnings seem sensible and well taken, though it is hard to see how Professor Gregory has committed these mistakes. It is perfectly clear that when the brain is said to 'see' or 'decode', no one is taken in by the metaphor to look for another eye, or another man. On the contrary, far from being blocked by the metaphor, inquiry does proceed to analyzing the next microstructural level of physical processes.

The stronger version of Kenny's charge against the 'homunculus fallacy' is more difficult to interpret, for it is not entirely clear what Kenny takes the fallacy to be, or what he would find

75

acceptable as an alternative mode of analysis. There are three possible interpretations of the stronger form of Kenny's diagnosis of the homunculus fallacy:

(1) It consists in extending the application of predicates from wholes to parts, where they can apply only metaphorically. If predicates having their primary application to wholes are taken to apply non-metaphorically to parts, a pseudo-explanation has been given and regression of explanations has begun.

(2) It consists in extending the application of predicates from organic wholes to their parts.

(3) It consists in extending predicates that apply to the activities of sentient, conscious organisms, and attributing them to states of the physical parts of organisms.

I want to discuss each of these separately, and then to say something about what seems to have led Kenny to take the position he adopts.

(1) If the fallacy consists in extending the application of predicates (or their synonyms) from wholes to the parts that compose them, then we could not explain the *cohesion* of compounds by a theory which postulates electro-magnetic *bonds* among elements. The repetition of a phrase, especially when it is used in quotes, or is given a technical meaning, does not always or necessarily involve either a pseudo-explanation or an infinite regress of explanations. For a fallacy to be committed, it is not enough that an expression describing the *explanandum* reappear in the *explanans*. It must have the same function in the whole theory that constitutes the explanations, as it has in describing the phenomena to be explained. Pseudo-explanations of the sort Kenny may have in mind occur only when the *explanans* and the *explanandum* are completely isomorphic, isolating exactly the same entities and processes, reproducing parallel structures of their operation. It is quite possible that the explanations of perception that Professor Gregory and his colleagues give of perception are isomorphic to the *explanandum*; but discovering the metaphoric repetition of a phrase is not sufficient to demonstrate isomorphism. Certainly Gregory's physiological analyses do not seem isomorphic to the behavior to be explained. Mapping the process of the excitation of optic nerves, and the 'transmission' of charges along the nerves, eventually showing how the optic nerves get connected with memory centers, language

centers and the motor system, does not *reproduce*, within the brain, the process of physical objects stimulating the optic nerve. Rather, it is an extended analysis of the *continuation* of that process.

Perhaps it is the use of the copula 'is' that gives the trouble here. On this interpretation of what Kenny finds fallacious in the homunculus argument, the difficulty seems to lie in saying that the activity *is* (nothing but) the micro-structural processes postulated to explain them. Suppose Professor Gregory were to drop the 'is', or rather were to expand it in such a way as to make it clear that he is not using it to imply an identity, but rather an identification. Would that take care of the problem? After all, in giving an explanation, one does say, in effect, 'And this *is* (an explanation of) . . .'

(2) If the fallacy consists in extending the application of predicates from organic wholes to their parts, we ought not to speak of the stomach as digesting or the lungs as breathing. Interpreted in this way, the homunculus argument, according to Kenny, really is a version of any reductivist or mechanistic explanation of the behavior of organisms. The fallacy is disguised by loose talk about 'associating' the behavior of organisms with certain physical states of its parts. Here again, one suspects that it is the copula that gives the primary difficulty, although there is also more at stake. On the one hand, Kenny is urging us not to take the construction of a mechanistic or neurological account of perception to *be* the conceptual or philosophical analysis of perception. So far so good. He is, in effect, telling us that we ought not to confuse the answer to one question ('What optical and neural processes take place when we see?') with the answer to another question ('What are the necessary and sufficient conditions for saying that someone has seen something?'). This confusion takes place, presumably, because the more general question, 'Under what conditions do we say that a person sees something?', can be interpreted either as requiring a scientific account of the visual processes, or as requiring a conceptual analysis of what it is to perceive. (We must ignore for the purposes of this discussion the problem of analyzing 'conceptual analyses'.)

Kenny takes what is proper and useful in his warning and extends it to contexts where its application appears question-begging or improper. For while he says that he is not against analyses of the sort that Gregory gives, but only against their being taken for *the* explanation, one wonders whether Kenny's animus isn't stronger than he says. What he seems to require is that the neuro-physiological analysis somehow reproduce or incorporate the organic character of the *explanandum*. Here Kenny seems to construct a dilemma that defeats any analysis. Either the explanatory theory will postulate entities and processes parallel to those mentioned in the explanation, or it will not. If it does postulate such processes, then some version of the 'homunculus fallacy' will be charged, and it will be said that either a vicious circle or an infinite regress has begun. If it does not postulate such processes, then the charge of 'reductivist analysis' will be levelled; it will be said that some essential characteristic of the process has been left out.

It is not clear what alternative forms of explanation Kenny would find acceptable. Having said that it is not the eye but the whole person that sees, and having established that seeing involves knowing and that knowing involves the capacity to behave in certain ways, *what* are we explainers to do next? It is also true that the whole person sleeps, and that it is not just a matter of the temperature lowering, the circulation slowing down and a characteristic pattern being registered on the EEG. Yet these are the conditions associated with sleeping. Even when we correct the vocabulary and say that it is the person who sees or sleeps, we still need to know how he does it. And we should go on giving just about the sorts of scientific explanations that Professor Gregory gives. It seems clear that Kenny does not want Gregory to stop what he is doing, but only to stop mislabeling it.

It is important to see that Kenny's argument can also be misunderstood and mislabelled. It might seem as though Kenny were saying: on the one hand there is a mechanistic account of the physical states 'associated' with seeing. These states can be explained scientifically. On the other hand, there is an activity of persons, called 'perceiving', which must be given quite a different sort of explanation. But if this move avoids the homunculus fallacy, it commits another mistake: that of multiplying processes. I am sure that Kenny doesn't mean to say that there are two distinct 'things', the activities of persons on the one hand, and the states of physical bodies on the other. Nor does he mean to say that the explanations of these two are distinct, and should be kept separate. But what he says can be misunderstood to imply that.

(3) If the fallacy consists in extending the application of predicates from sentient, conscious wholes to their parts, we ought not to speak of hands grasping or holding, since only persons can have the sorts of intentions which are pre-conditions for the legitimate application of such expressions. Kenny charges Descartes with having succumbed to this form of the fallacy, though Descartes himself clearly diagnosed the nature of the error involved. One hesitates to disagree with Kenny on matters involving the interpretation of Descartes, yet I wonder whether the sort of distinction that Kenny wants to make, between knowing as having-the-capacity-to-use-information and 'knowing' as being-in-a-state-of-containing-information, isn't just the sort of distinction that Descartes *is* making when he slips into talking about the way in which the radiation of retinal images affects the pineal gland. He is describing the physical *states* that are associated with 'having information', and saying that these are different from the *activities* the soul exercises when it knows something clearly and distinctly. That this distinction leads Descartes into difficulties should give us pause in making the capacity-state distinction as sharply as Kenny wants to make it. Once the distinction has been made, it will still be necessary to identify the physical processes 'associated' with the exercise of the capacities, and the question of the analysis of the identificatory copula will arise all over again. Having given an Aristotelian analysis of the activities of persons, we may, and indeed should ask, what psycho-physical states are associated with these various capacities.

Part of Kenny's argument for introducing the 'whole' person into the analysis of perception—and I think incidentally, no one would quarrel with him on this point, properly understood—is that our criteria for whether a person has seen something, and perhaps even our determination of what it is that he has seen, involves observing the complex behavior of a person over a period of time. But we must distinguish the criteria for determining whether someone has seen something (or trying to describe what he's seen) from an analysis of the mechanism or process of perception. Someone might hold the extreme view that once we have a really good neuro-physiological account of the mechanisms of perception, we could tell whether and possibly even what (although this seems more questionable) a subject has seen by having him wired up appropriately, without observing the person's adaptive behavior in natural situations. Suppose as a matter of experimental fact, it turned out that there is a strikingly high correlation between the neurophysiologist's attribution of perception to subjects and our attribution of perceptual experiences following the sorts of criteria Kenny would prefer us to use. Kenny's point is that even if the neurophysiologist's account has strong predictive power, his explanation should not tempt us to saying that the brain *sees*. That warning does indeed seem proper, but it does not follow that the neurophysiologist hasn't given an explanation of the process. What after all is *the* explanation? Perhaps what is wrong on both sides is the supposition that there is a privileged question, and a privileged reply. Would we say that a properly Aristotelian account of the activity of the whole person in perception gives *the* explanation of perception?

The utility of Kenny's warning lies in his distinguishing a conceptual analysis from a scientific explanation. Having made that distinction, Kenny does not of course claim to analyze the relation of the two types of explanation to one another or to give us criteria for when expressions can be imported from one type of explanation to another. Kenny has also shown that some of the predicates that properly pertain only to the activities of persons are likely to mislead us into asking the wrong sorts of questions if they are applied to states of physical bodies, and vice versa. He has not, however, given us general criteria for determining when such extensions are going to be misleading and when they are not. I do not believe that general criteria for this can be given; it is thus misleading to talk about 'fallacies' in this area, where we have only good sense to guide us.

REPLY TO MRS RORTY

Anthony J. P. Kenny

I wish to disown several of the theses which are attributed to me (more or less tentatively) by Professor Rorty. First, I do not accuse Professor Gregory of mistaking mechanistic description for conceptual analysis; nor do I think that either the philosopher's answer or the neurophysiologist's answer to the question 'what is perception?' enjoys a privileged status. Secondly, I do not object to every extension of the application of a predicate from a sentient whole to its parts. Thirdly, I took up no position on the general question whether conscious activities can be said to *be* (nothing but) the micro-structural processes postulated to explain them. I will expand each of these points, and then briefly restate why I call the homunculus fallacy a fallacy.

I do not think that Gregory is under any illusion that he is doing conceptual analysis. I think he is engaged in constructing, and testing experimentally, hypotheses about the mechanisms necessary to explain the phenomena of visual perception. But conceptual analysis is relevant to what he is doing in two ways. First, analysis of the concept of *perception* is necessary to delimit what are the phenomena to be explained; secondly, analysis of the concepts of *sight* and *language* show that such things as seeing and decoding cannot be done by brains unless we can attribute to brains certain types of behaviour which we can attribute to whole human beings. To attribute such activities to brains without suggesting how the relevant behaviour might be attributable to brains is, I maintained, to mask empirical problems which remain to be solved.

The moral of my paper, I said, was not that human-being predicates cannot have their use extended at all, but that their use must be extended cautiously. Consequently, I am unmoved when Mrs Rorty points out that hands can grasp and hold: such

81

extensions seem to me well within the bounds of caution. More-over, my objection was not essentially to predicates of wholes being attached to predicates of parts, but to predicates belonging to human beings being attached to non-human beings. The same fallacy could be committed (though my name for it would not be apt) by the incautious application of human-being predicates to wholes of which human beings are parts, such as communities and states. Populations, like human beings, grow and shrink; but it would obviously be fallacious to argue that a human being was shrinking because the population he belongs to is shrinking, or that a population is growing because every member of it is growing. And states may have intentions which none of their citizens have.[1]

The question whether perception can be said to be *identical* with physiological processes seems to me to lack a clear sense, and I do not wish to answer it one way or the other. My com-plaint against Gregory's identification of visual perception with his postulated selection of internal models was not based on a general thesis that perception cannot be identical with a brain process. Though states and capacities are conceptually different, it need not be misleading to say, e.g. that a peg's ability to fit into round holes *is* its roundness. In the same way, it may be that there is a physiological process—the acquisition of a physio-logical state—which can be said to *be* visual perception. But no one can claim to have identified such a process until he has brought out its connection with the types of behaviour which are the criteria for the occurrence of visual perception. And this Gregory has not done.

A fallacy, strictly speaking, is a form of argument which can lead from true premises to a false conclusion. The inappropriate use of predicates, not being a form of argument, is not strictly a fallacy, as I observed in my paper. But it leads to a form of argument, which I claimed to detect in Gregory's articles, which *is* fallacious in the strict sense of the word: the argument that because a certain human-being predicate attaches to a human being it attaches to his brain, or *vice versa*. The mere inap-propriate use of human-being predicates may be called a fallacy in an extended sense, because it may suggest conclusions which are unjustified: notably the conclusion that more has been ex-plained by a psychological theory than has in fact been explained.

ANTHONY J. P. KENNY

Normally, in an adult human being, the ability to see carries with it the ability to say what is seen, though of course not everything which is actually seen is actually talked about. The use of language to report what is seen, like any use of language, is remarkably free from stimulus control—a point which has been repeatedly made, in general terms, by Chomsky. No account of human perception can approach adequacy unless it includes an explanation of this fact. Consequently, even if we knew every detail of the physiological processes by which visual information reaches the brain, and every detail of the physiological processes by which the linguistic utterance of visual reports is produced, the problem of the relationship between the input and the output would be completely untouched. This problem is a major part of the problem of the physiological explanation of perception, and its existence is masked by talk of the brain reading features of objects from images and calling up appropriate muscle power.

REFERENCE

[1] *Cf.* L. Wittgenstein, *Zettel* (tr. G. E. M. Anscombe), Oxford: Basil Blackwell, 1967, pp. 1–48.

5

BEHAVIOR, BELIEF AND EMOTION

Alasdair C. MacIntyre

Dr Kenny has been arguing in defense of whole persons against a seeming dissection of them, in which, by a kind of pseudo-substitution, their parts are made to play the place of pseudo-wholes. Professor MacIntyre here argues against another fallacious identification, made primarily by psychologists and social scientists, a confusion of personal experience and action with its observable expression. His paper defends the liberation of personal emotions, feelings and beliefs from their identification with 'behavior' in the sense of their continent observable expressions.

Like Taylor and Kenny, he is concerned with the contrast between persons and their intentions, on the one hand, and some surrogate for these, in his case 'behavior', on the other. His argument takes us, as we shall see, a firm step further forward in the debate. For although behavior is not *mere* movement nor *mere* causal sequences of neural events, the concept 'behavior' as used in psychology or sometimes in sociology is still reductive. It still denotes substantially *less* than the reality with which it purports to deal.

I want in this paper to make a few points that are relevant to the controversies about behaviorism. What is to be meant by behaviorism? This, oddly enough, I do not need to specify precisely since my arguments, if correct, hold against *anything* that it would be worth calling behaviorism. Consider for example the following theses about the emotion of resentment:

(1) 'Smith resents what Jones did' means the same as some specifiable statement or set of statements about Smith's behavior.

(2) 'Smith resents what Jones did' is true, if and only if some specifiable statement or set of statements about Smith's behavior is true.

(3) Although 'Smith resents what Jones did' does not mean

the same as some statement or set of statements about Smith's behavior, there is nothing more to Smith's feeling resentful than that Smith behaved and was disposed to behave in certain specifiable ways.

(4) Although it is not the case that 'Smith resents what Jones did' is true, if and only if some specifiable statement or set of statements about Smith's behavior is true, it is the case that if it is true that 'Smith resents what Jones did' is true, then either some specifiable statement or set of statements about Smith's behavior is true or else some special explanation is necessary as to why the behavior which, if it had occurred, would have made that statement or those statements true did not occur.

These theses are importantly different. The truth of (1) entails the truth of (2), but not *vice versa*; the truth of (3) entails the truth of (2), but the falsity of (1); and the truth of (4) entails the falsity of (1), (2) and (3). But, different as they are, they all have in common the following thesis: that there is a connection between the emotion of resentment and certain specific and specifiable forms of behavior such that, even if there is more to resentment than the exhibition of the behavior in question, and even if resentment may be felt without the behavior in question being exhibited, nonetheless behavior of that specific kind is the-behavior-which-is-exhibited-when-resentment-is-expressed-in-behavior. I understand this thesis in such a way that it entails first that the connection between behavior and emotion is not merely contingent, as the connection between a twitching of my ear and my feeling resentment might be—it might just happen to be the case that whenever I feel resentment my ear twitches—and secondly that there are a limited and specifiable number of forms of behavior in which and through which resentment may be exhibited. It is precisely this last point that I wish to deny, and the argument of the first section of this paper will be directed to showing that resentment and some other emotions may be expressed by any form of behavior whatsoever, and that there is therefore no necessary connection between some emotions at least and particular forms of behavior.

1

A man who yesterday chatted pleasantly with an academic

colleague today crosses the street to avoid meeting him. Why? He has in the interval read a review of his latest book by this colleague and resents what he takes to be his unjust verdict. He expresses his resentment by crossing the road. Suppose that he knew that this colleague had a peculiar love of a rare fruit which he could only procure at one store; he might then buy up the entire stock of that fruit and so express his resentment. Or suppose that he knows that what his colleague prizes is an invitation to a particular party; he might then express his resentment by intercepting the invitation. Crossing a road, buying fruit, stealing mail; these actions have nothing in common with each other and yet they can all express resentment. Precisely because there is no characteristic which they have to possess in order to function as expressions of resentment, precisely because, except as possible expressions of resentment, there is no reason for including these items in the list rather than any others, it seems plausible to suppose that any action whatsoever can function as an expression of resentment.

Consider now three possible criticisms of this argument. Surely, it might be argued, all such items of behavior do fall under some one single description other than 'resentful'; they are all, for example, items of *hostile* behavior. This is of course true, but it does not affect my point. First of all, just as any action at all can be an expression of resentment, any action at all can be a hostile action. Crossing a road, buying fruit, stealing mail can all be hostile in specific contexts, just as they can be resentful in specific contexts. To this, it might be objected that there are some actions which could not by their very nature be hostile, if by that is meant 'directed to the harm of others'; how could suicide be in this sense hostile? The answer is of course that there is a well-recognized class of suicides, the so-called 'revenge' suicides ('I'll kill myself, and *that* will teach them a lesson'), where the point of the suicide is precisely that it is a hostile action. Moreover the variety of types of action which can be characterized as expressions of resentment can only be characterized as hostile just because 'hostile' is partially synonymous with resentful, because resentment is a species of hostility. So that the fact that we can find another description under which all these actions fall does not go any way to show that we have found an additional common characteristic shared by all these actions.

86

A second objection to my thesis might be that I am able to understand all these actions as expressions of resentment only by establishing a context of a given kind. It is not crossing the road or buying fruit or stealing mail that is the expression of resentment, but crossing-the-road-to-avoid-speaking-to-some-one-who-has-unjustly-criticized-me or buying-fruit-specially-desired-by-someone-who-has-unjustly-criticized-me and so on. This is in a way correct. We are only able to construe the actions in question as behavior expressive of resentment by connecting them with the reasons that the agent has for doing what he does. But these reasons cannot be identified with what the agent does, nor are they exhibited in doing what he does. Certainly it is only because the action is done for a certain kind of reason that it is an expression of resentment. But to say this is to say that *qua* action and *qua* the action that it is, the relation between the action and the resentment is purely contingent. To make the point in this way does perhaps help us to understand better why many philosophers may have thought otherwise. They may have envisaged the action under some description, such as the descriptions above, which links the action to the reason for performing it and passed from asserting truly that such a description is conceptually connected with the characterization of the emotion in question as resentment to asserting falsely that the action itself was not merely contingently connected to the resentment.

A third point might be raised not so much as an objection to my initial thesis as an objection to drawing possibly illegitimate conclusions from it. For it might be suggested that while what I have said is true of the emotion of resentment, it is not true of emotions in general. What is special about the emotion of resentment? A man cannot be said to resent something unless he has a particular type of belief. He must believe that he has been wronged in the light of what it is established that a man in his position has a right to expect. Unless he has such a belief what he feels may be characterized perhaps as anger, but not as resentment. What then of anger? Is there some belief which a man who is said to be angry must possess? It is clearly the case that usually and characteristically a man who is angry believes that something has been done that is harmful to or an affront to himself or his interests or those about whom he cares. But is it not sometimes the case that a man just feels angry? And does not anger therefore perhaps differ in a not irrelevant way from resentment?

The relevance of this point to the argument is as follows. In the case of resentment it is because the circumstances, tastes and other relevant characteristics of the person against whom resentment is directed are indefinitely variable that the actions which may express that resentment are indefinitely variable. Hence the indefinite variability of the actions which express resentment is connected with the belief which a man to whom resentment is correctly ascribed must possess. But if in the case of anger there is no such belief, then may not anger be connected with behavior expressive of anger in some way quite different from that in which resentment is connected with behavior expressive of resentment?

It is important to stress first that where anger is divorced from the belief that usually and characteristically accompanies it, namely the belief that some identifiable person has done some identifiable harm, we are confronted not with anger as it basically is, with the emotion in a pure form, so to speak, but rather with an uncharacteristic and marginal case, which is less easily intelligible to us than anger in its usual form and which we understand by its resemblance to these forms. (Try to imagine a culture in which everyone is all the time in a rage with no one in particular about nothing in particular, but is never angry with specific individuals about specific harms. I am inclined to think that we would treat this as a different emotion.)

Secondly anger in these special cases is not in fact unaccompanied by belief; it is just that the belief is expressed in sentences containing more variables. The belief that someone or anyone has done something harmful or affronting to me, although I know not whom or what, is still a belief, and the belief that connects the feelings accompanying it to other feelings of anger. Hence anger, like resentment, is connected with a belief and, although the belief is a less complex one, the persons or actions against whom anger is directed are as indefinitely variable as are the objects of resentment. Hence also the forms of behavior by means of which anger too may be expressed are indefinitely variable.

I take it therefore that the lack of any necessary connection between emotion and behavior holds in the case of anger as well as in that of resentment. But if anger and resentment resemble each other in this way, how do they differ? It seems plausible to suggest that the only difference is in the beliefs of the agents in question. The emotion of anger involves the belief that someone has done harm or has affronted me or my interests or those about whom I care—whether deserved or not; that of resentment, the belief that someone has done undeserved harm or offered an undeserved affront to me or my interests. The difference is not in the phenomenological feel of the two emotions: introspective reports do not reveal different sensations in the case of anger from those present in the case of resentment. Nor is the difference in the behavior through which each is expressed, since each may be expressed in the same behavior. The beliefs alone provide a difference.

To this it may be retorted that the relationship of anger to resentment is a special case. For after all resentment is a species of anger. It may therefore be true that the felt quality of the emotion and the behavior do not differ in this case; but if instead of asking for the difference between anger and resentment, we were to enquire what is the difference between anger and elation or between resentment and gratitude the same would not hold. Consider resentment and gratitude. To feel grateful is to feel pleased that someone has done more for your good or for the good of those about whom you care than you had a right to expect. But like resentment any kind of behavior may express gratitude; the fact that one emotion is one of pleasure in something and the other of displeasure at something does not entail that the very same behavior may not express gratitude which expresses resentment. If I am grateful to you for what you have done and I know that you resent what someone else has done, I may express my gratitude to you by doing to him what if you did it to him would express your resentment. Hence the difference between gratitude and resentment is not a difference in behavior. I take it that it is also not a difference in the felt quality of inner states. The feelings of a man in the extremity of an emotion such as gratitude is customarily described by novelists in ways that are remarkably like the ways in which the feelings of a man in the extremity of an emotion such as fear are described. His throat goes dry, his temples throb, his pulse rate rises, his eyes prick with tears and so on. The physiological symptoms of emotion seem remarkably constant, and the physiologists seem to agree with the novelists about this.

If I conclude then that the difference between emotions lies in the belief and not in the behavior, I cannot possibly identify emotions with patterns of behavior. But a behaviorist might try at this point to recover his position by an argument of more general import. For he might contend that the notion of belief itself is to be analyzed in terms of behavior, asserting that 'X believes that p' is logically equivalent to or means the same as 'X has a disposition to manifest certain patterns of behavior' and also that to manifest a belief is to manifest patterns of behavior, so that the appropriate evidence which would warrant the assertion that 'X believes that p' is that X has on occasion exhibited the relevant behavior. In order for these assertions to be defensible the behavior in question would have to include what X says as well as what X does, what some behaviorists have quaintly called 'linguistic behavior'. More specifically it is what X asserts and not just what X says which has to be included in the list of relevant items: unless on certain types of possible occasions a man was prepared to assert that p and to deny that not p, he could not be said to believe that p. It follows therefore that if the notion of belief is to be analyzed in terms of behavior, the behavior in terms of which it is analyzed must include acts of assertion and denial. But now what is it to assert that p? It is to give one's hearers or readers to understand that one believes that p and that p is worthy of belief. That is to say, the notion of assertion has to be explained by referring to the notion of belief. So it turns out that the notion of belief has not been analyzed in terms of behavior, for the type of behavior to which reference has to be made in the course of the analysis can itself only be understood by referring to the concept of belief. The concept of belief is at least as fundamental a concept, and possibly a more fundamental concept, than that of behavior.

To this it might be answered that to assert and to deny *are* just forms of behavior. There is clearly a sense in which this is true. If I say of someone that he behaved disgracefully in denying that he was to blame, I say something intelligible to every user of standard English. But in this idiomatic sense of 'behavior', we cannot give a behaviorist account even of behavior. For to assert of someone that he asserts that p is to go beyond saying that he utters the sentence 'p' even if he did in fact assert that p by uttering the sentence 'p'. It is to construe his utterance in terms of his intention in uttering the sentence. The intentions that inform that utterance, like all intentions, presuppose beliefs. So that we have once again, in the course of trying to analyze the concept of belief, been brought back to it.

Finally it ought to be noticed that in discussing behaviorism I have not ascribed to the behaviorist that extreme view which equates behavior with physical movement. When I argued that there are at least certain emotions which can be expressed by any behavior whatsoever, my examples—those of crossing the road, buying fruit and stealing mail—were all examples of actions, and their descriptions were descriptions which specified an intention embodied in what was done. If the behaviorist wants to insist that he means more than this by behavior, that in his view behavior has not yet been characterized adequately until it is characterized by the emotions it expresses, if any, and that therefore resentful behavior for example is just a species of behavior and not behavior informed by something other than that behavior, namely an emotion, his thesis becomes trivial. If he wants on the other hand to insist that he means less than this by 'behavior', perhaps equating behavior with physical movement, then my preceding arguments hold with as great or greater force than they do against behavior equated with human action.

The outcome of my arguments is then that behavior stands in indirect and complex relationship to emotions. Without accepting classical introspectionism, we admit that the introspectionist, and indeed ordinary language usage, according to which we speak of emotions as lying behind behavior and as being concealed as much as revealed by it, does not seem exaggerated. But if this is so what are we to say about our knowledge of the emotions of others? How far can we know what they feel?

2

Paul Ziff in his 'About Behaviorism' considers the contention that 'You can in principle if not in fact always find out whether or not I am behaving in certain ways. But you cannot even in principle always find out whether or not I am angry.'[1] and even waiving all difficulties about the locution 'you can in principle find out' finds what he takes to be two fatal objections to it. One which I shall not consider, since I agree with it, is that it is false that you can in principle always find out how I am behaving. The other objection he puts as follows: 'You can in principle always find out whether or not I am angry because I can tell you. Hence you need attend only to my verbal behavior. (I assume that it would be generally odd to speak of my being mistaken about whether or not I am angry.) To suppose that you cannot in principle find out whether or not I am angry would be to suppose that I cannot in principle tell you whether or not I am angry. I find such a supposition unintelligible.'[2] Agreeing with finding this last supposition unintelligible, I still want to disagree with the main point.

From the fact that, if I *am* angry, I can always tell you that I am angry, it does not follow that from what I say you can always tell if I *am* angry or not. The reason for this is that I can always deceive you by lying or otherwise misleading you and that I can always simply refuse to reveal what I feel. The use of 'can in principle', which Ziff over-generously takes over from the anti-behaviorists whom he is criticizing, is one source of trouble. For it may lead us to concede not only that I may always when angry tell you that I am, but also that your knowledge of my anger is unproblematic. But it isn't.

When Ziff talks of verbal behavior he may be suggesting that what I say about my emotions stands to my emotions in the same relationship that the behavior which expresses my emotions stands to my emotions. But this is surely false either on a behaviorist or on a non-behaviorist view. On a behaviorist view it is false because, on that view, my having an emotion consists in my exhibiting a certain pattern of behavior. The behavior which expresses the emotion is the emotion. But when I tell you what I feel I do not express the emotion, I report it. Or rather I may or may not be expressing the emotion in the act of reporting it, but I am certainly reporting it. This is partly a matter of to whom I am speaking. If I am angry with you and I say 'I am angry with you', I am doubtless expressing my anger in the act of reporting it. But if I am angry with you and say to someone else 'I am angry with Smith' then it would be odd to say that I was expressing my anger. It is, in any case, utterances and neither sentences nor statements that are expressive of emotion, and utterances

92

may certainly stand to an emotion just as other behavior stands to it. But what I say when I so utter does not stand in the same relationship to the emotion.

There is no asymmetry, so far as emotions are concerned (and if I restrict the point to emotions in this paper this must not be taken to imply that I hold different views about sensations) between first person sentences, on the one hand, and second and third person sentences, on the other, or between statements expressed by means of first person sentences and statements expressed by means of second and third person sentences. I take it that to understand personal pronouns at least two conditions must be satisfied: first, no one understands personal pronouns who does not understand that they are blanks for which personal proper names may be substituted. I do not understand personal pronouns when I am unable to make the inference from hearing someone say 'MacIntyre is drunk' to 'He is saying that I am drunk.' To have understood this is to be able to see what is wrong with attempts to suggest that for 'I' what can be substituted is not a proper name but a description such as 'the present speaker'. Of course first person statements can often be correctly paraphrased by statements using such expressions as 'the present speaker'. But 'the present speaker' is not necessarily self-referential in the way that 'I' is. While I am speaking someone may say 'The present speaker is drunk' and he would not normally be taken to mean that he is drunk, but that I am, while, if I hear someone say, 'MacIntyre is drunk', I must if I understand him see that it follows that if what he says is true then I am drunk, but I do not need to have even learnt the use of the expression 'the present speaker' to understand 'I' and to use it correctly.

Secondly it is a condition of my understanding personal pronouns that I understand that if I say truly of you that 'you are drunk' then you are able to say truly of yourself (provided that you are not too drunk—perhaps this is what 'can in principle' means) 'I am drunk' and I can say truly of you to a third person 'he is drunk' *and* in addition that if you say truly of me that 'you are drunk' then I can say truly of myself 'I am drunk' and so on. In other words to have extricated oneself from the egocentric predicament—in so far as this is a matter of grammar rather than of beliefs—is a necessary condition for the exercise of the

93

ability to use those parts of speech which are held by some philosophers to generate it.

It is these facts about personal pronouns which make it clear that if the sentence 'MacIntyre is angry' can be used truly to make a statement about me, then 'I am angry' can be used by me to make the same true statement. This statement is, let us say, on this particular occasion true, but it could have been false. The statement made by my saying 'I am angry' truly is thus a statement which stands in the same relationship to my anger that the statement 'MacIntyre is angry' said by someone else stands to it. But if this is so then the *statement* cannot be an expression of my anger, let alone the sentence. Certainly I may so utter the sentence 'I am angry' with clenched lips, gnashing teeth and all the conventional accompaniments of anger, whatever they are, in such a way that my utterance is an expression of my anger. But my utterance of '$E = mc^2$' can be an expression of my anger in just the same way as my utterance of 'I am angry.'

It is not to the point that I cannot be mistaken about whether MacIntyre is angry if I am MacIntyre. I cannot be mistaken because I cannot fail to have all the necessary evidence for what I assert. But whenever I have all the necessary evidence for what I assert, I cannot be mistaken either. Placed with vision unimpaired in front of a tray containing a bottle and two glasses, I cannot be mistaken in asserting that here are a bottle and two glasses. Yet of course in both cases, although I cannot be mistaken as to what is true and what is false, I can of course knowingly assert what is false. Hence Ziff's acknowledgement that sometimes at least I can only know whether you are angry if you will tell me, entails that I cannot know whether you are angry or not unless I know that you are a trustworthy reporter of your emotions. But can I ever know this?

It is not just that a great deal of behavior does not bear its meaning on its face and that we cannot tell what intentions inform it simply by observing it, because it is susceptible of more than one and perhaps of many interpretations. But behavior which is *qua* behavior unambiguous can be put to the service of a pretence, just as assertions can be lies. This is the point at which to note that when behaviorists have assimilated what I say to my behavior, using such expressions as 'linguistic behavior' or 'verbal behavior' they have been wrong not so much in that they assimilated than as in that they tried to reduce uses of language to forms of behavior instead of seeing that certain forms of behavior are best understood as at least resembling uses of language. One reason why one of the key positions of this paper has not been accepted by some philosophers, namely the position that any behavior at all can be expressive of certain emotions at least, is that there is a behavioral iconography of emotion. That is, there are certain forms of behavior which are by convention understood to symbolize the presence of a particular emotion. To exhibit such behavior is equivalent to saying 'I am angry' (or whatever emotion is in question). It is because of this symbolic character of such behavior—of shaking the fist and clenching the teeth in relation to anger, for example—that it can be put to different uses just as speech can. In Japan and Korea there is a tradition of visiting a recently bereaved person who will then laugh and joke with his guests without making reference to the bereavement. The host by doing this asserts to his guests that he does not wish to burden them with his grief; the guests assert in reply that they would not wish to burden the host with the belief that he has in fact burdened them with his grief. It is the conventional, symbolic character of the behavior that makes this possible. So far as this iconographic aspect of behavior is concerned, the conventions could, of course, be other than they are. We could express anger by touching our toes or gratitude by performing cartwheels. If it is objected to this that very often the behaviour expressive of anger or gratitude is evoked from us by some action, is not a voluntary, deliberate, or controlled response, it must be pointed out that very often too what we say about our emotions is similarly evoked. An involuntary utterance of a statement about my behavior does not, because it is involuntary, lose its conventional character. So too with behavior symbolic of emotion.

There is, of course, a difference between speech and such symbolic behavior which ought to be noted. I cannot use such behavior to indicate to you that I am angry without being taken to have expressed and not merely indicated the fact of my anger. But this difference does not affect the preceding argument. What follows from that argument is that whether I say to you that I am angry or show you that I am angry I may be misleading you, and from this two further consequences follow. The first is that over large areas I can sometimes have no way of knowing what you feel. Any performance of behavior by you no matter how extended may be a pretence at the service of some further unrevealed intention and emotion. This gap between performed behavior on the one hand and intention and emotion on the other is what goes unnoticed in a sociological perspective such as Erving Goffman's in which there is nothing to human beings but their performance of the behavior appropriate to different roles and the behavior (equally and in precisely the same way rule-governed) necessary to produce the behavior appropriate to the roles. I introduce the doctrines of Goffman in *The Presentation of The Self in Everyday Life*[3] at this point because in identifying what is omitted from an account of social situations which is restricted to overt performances I have identified not merely what is omitted from this particular piece of sociological enquiry and description, but what it is at once essential and very difficult to include. The early behaviorists believed that their doctrine provided the only basis for a scientific knowledge of human beings and believed that such knowledge could have a firmer basis than our everyday knowledge of each other has. Goffman resembles them in believing that the notion of 'a true self' behind the role-and-rule-governed performances is an anti-scientific myth perpetrated by those who, as he puts it, wish to keep part of the human world safe from sociology. But in liquidating the distinction between the self and its performances Goffman loses sight of the way in which we can only take what others do seriously if we trust what they say on certain key occasions.

It is not just then that the possibility of deception and of being misled are so large; it is also that our beliefs about others have to be founded so largely on trust if the preceding arguments are correct. I may argue on an inductive basis about other people's emotions in so far as these are not exhibited in or deducible from their behavior; but however well-contrived my inductive learning policies are, the evidence from which I argue will include at crucial points what others have said, and my willingness to treat what they have said as trustworthy or untrustworthy cannot itself be inductively based. Why not? Could I not learn that Smith is generally trustworthy and so be entitled to argue that I can expect him to be trustworthy about his inner life too? The problem here is that we could only derive well-founded inductive generalizations about the connection between a man's trustworthiness in his monetary transactions, say, and his trustworthiness in reporting his emotions if we already had independent access to his emotions; and we do not. Every piece of behavior is open to doubt. Does this entail skepticism about the emotions of others? Or to compare the not quite ridiculous with the not completely sublime does my conclusion about the emotions of other people resemble Kant's conclusion about God: that the removal of knowledge has left room for faith?

To put matters like this would be unhelpful; for clearly faith in God is something that is dispensable. It is indeed of the essence of faith that one can fail to have it. But if our beliefs about other people depend upon a presumption of their trustworthiness, so that there is indeed a moral element in our beliefs about others—and those who have wanted to mark a difference in this respect between our knowledge of nature and our knowledge of others have thus been right—it is not the case that we can rationally decide not to make this presumption. For emotions are not occurrences in the lives of individuals, insulated from similar occurrences in the lives of other individuals. As Hume points out in his discussion of sympathy in the *Treatise* what I feel is in large part a response to what I take others to feel or not feel. You are resentful of my lack of gratitude at your generosity in the face of my anger at your lack of sympathy for my depression over your sentimentality. Such chains of emotion are characteristic of the emotional life; the plot of a novel often traces just such a chain. It follows that systematic skeptical doubt about the emotions of others, based on an acknowledgement of the opaque quality of their behavior and a refusal to trust their avowals, would produce an inability to respond to others, for we would not know to what to respond, and the beliefs that inform our emotions would not specify adequate intentional objects for our emotions. We have to trust one another at this basic level or be paralyzed in our humanity. This is not a choice.

There is one final point worth attending to. Small children exhibit certain emotions spontaneously before they have learned to pretend, and about their emotions animals never learn to pretend. So in these cases the element of trust in avowals is obviously absent. Rage is an example of this. Small children also sometimes learn in the case of certain other emotions to exhibit behavior symbolically expressive of the emotion before they have learned to feel the emotion. This is often true in the case of gratitude. But what they have to learn in order to exhibit adult emotions involves them in learning how to pretend, how to be ironic, how to lie and how to produce the stock responses which sustain fatigued human relationships. In so doing they become, like the adult world, opaque. Behaviorists were in the right when they stressed that sometimes we want to claim that we can recognize what others are feeling better than they can; but in repudiating what introspectionists seemed to imply, that we are all continually opaque to each other all the time, they may have underrated the extent to which we are very often opaque to each other a great deal of the time. Misunderstanding and not understanding are at the core of human life, a fact perhaps standing in the way of the projects of scientific enquiry about human beings, even if we view it as an obstacle to be circumvented rather than as a final barrier. This conclusion I find disconcerting. But perhaps the nature of reality is such that we ought to have learnt by now never to be disconcerted at being disconcerted.

REFERENCES

[1] Paul Ziff, 'About Behaviorism' in *Philosophic Turnings*, Ithaca: Cornell University Press, 1966, pp. 155–60, 157.
[2] *Loc. cit.*
[3] Erving Goffman, *The Presentation of The Self in Everyday Life*, Garden City, New York: Doubleday, 1959.

6

THE CRITIQUE OF ARTIFICIAL REASON*

Hubert Dreyfus

'Mechanism', it was pointed out earlier, has two senses: the second sense mentioned of a 'mechanistic world view', and the more literal sense of a 'mechanism', a 'mechanical' device or operational technique. In the former sense, 'mechanism' is reductivism, the monolithic one-level ontology which all the papers here collected seek in one way or another to modify or oppose. From the point of view of either Prigogine or Grene, however, 'mechanisms' already resist reduction; Prigogine argues that organized structures need physical laws of *organization*, not of entropy only, to explain their genesis and operation, Grene argues, following Polanyi, that living things as machines already transcend physics, since they demand both physicochemical and engineering principles for their explanation. Taylor, moreover, concedes still more to the biological 'mechanist' in arguing that even wholly reductive ('mechanistic' = physicochemical) explanations would still permit adequate reference either to intentional descriptions or even to intentional explanations of human action and conscious life systematically correlated with them. Kenny, in turn, warning against the dangers of such attempts, may be found to suggest the need for a more all-embracing anti-reductivism. But MacIntyre's argument reveals more clearly the need for a radically new position. For although behavior is 'mechanism' in the engineering sense, and so not mere physics or physiology, it is not yet personal. The resistance to reduction adumbrated by the previous essayists had not yet faced this issue. For them, reductivism has

*EDITOR'S NOTE: This article is the text of the annual Suarez Lecture delivered at Fordham University, 29 April 1968 and was originally published by *Thought* (43, 1968, pp. 507–22) which gave us permission to reproduce it here.

AUTHOR'S NOTE: This work was supported in part by the National Science Foundation under Grant GS 1953. Earlier versions of this paper were read at Indiana University and Northwestern University. I am indebted to participants in those discussions for helpful suggestions. Copyright 1968 by Hubert L. Dreyfus.

already been resisted when we exhibit the untenability of a one-level metaphysic of matter-in-motion. For MacIntyre, however, one conjectures, the reduction of persons to their observable behavior is a form of reductivism, not its confutation.

This is the issue faced by Professor Dreyfus. So far as living things are machines, the earlier argument runs (though of course this does not mean that they are wholly so), they are already resistant to physico-chemical reduction. But for Professor Dreyfus the identification of minds with machines is precisely the reductivism he finds it imperative to defeat. His argument therefore takes us another and a long step in the direction of a more comprehensive anti-reductive view. Men are not closed systems explicable by the second law; they are structured, organized beings, to be explained by the laws of far from equilibrium physics as well (Prigogine). Men are not mere physical systems: they are functioning systems, needing engineering principles as well for their explication (Grene). Men are not mere machines, or behavior sequences; they are persons, characterized by the intentionality of their experience (in various perspectives, Taylor, Kenny, MacIntyre). In so far therefore as men are intentional beings, they are not machines, not stuff for engineers to tinker with. The nature of minds or persons can be understood only in the light of a metaphysic (and one should add, an epistemology) which transcends technology. So argues Dreyfus.

In a recent book on the mathematical theory of computers, Marvin Minsky, one of the leading workers in Artificial Intelligence (AI), gave voice to the optimism guiding his research and that of others in the field:

> Within a generation, I am convinced, few compartments of intellect will remain outside the machine's realm—the problem of creating 'artificial intelligence' will be substantially solved.[1]

In so far as this is a prediction, one way to find out whether it is accurate is simply to wait a generation and see. But in so far as the prediction is presented as a conviction, we, as philosophers, may want to ask whether this conviction is well-founded.

Minsky is typical of workers in the area in giving two sorts of argument in support of his view: (1) Empirical arguments based on progress achieved thus far, and (2) *A priori* arguments about what machines can, in principle, do. It might seem at first sight that these are two distinct sorts of argument and that philosophers should concern themselves only with the *a priori* ones, but the truism that experimental data are meaningless until interpreted is especially applicable in this new, and barely scientific, area of inquiry. What we take the data to mean depends upon our assumptions, so that the empirical arguments implicitly reflect the *a priori* ones. It will therefore be my contention that the optimism underlying work in AI is unjustified *both* on empirical and *a priori* grounds. I will argue that the empirical arguments supporting it gain their plausibility only on the basis of an appeal to an implicit philosophical assumption, and that this assumption, far from being justified, simply perpetuates a fundamental error of the Western philosophical tradition.

1

Language translation, or the use of computers to simulate the understanding of natural languages, offers the clearest illustration of how optimistic assumptions have enabled enthusiasts to interpret as promising, data which is ambiguous, to say the least. Minsky cites as encouraging evidence of progress the existence of 'machines that handle abstract-nonmathematical problems and *deal with ordinary-language expressions*'.[2] Admittedly, 'deal with' is rather vague, but in another article Minsky comes right out and says of a program for solving algebra word problems, Bobrow's STUDENT, that 'it understands English'.[3] In fact this program embodies nothing one would ever want to call syntactic or semantic understanding. It simply breaks up the sentences into units on the basis of cues such as the words 'times', 'of', 'equal', and so on, equates these sentence chunks with xs and ys, and tries to set up simultaneous equations. If these equations cannot be solved, it appeals to further rules for breaking up the sentences into other units and tries again. The whole scheme works only because there is the constraint, not present in understanding ordinary discourse, that the pieces of the sentence, when represented by variables, will set up soluble equations. Such a program is so far from semantic understanding that, as Bobrow admits, it would interpret 'The number of times I went to the movies' as the product of two variables: 'the number of' and 'I went to the movies', because 'times' is always interpreted as an operator indicating multiplication.[4]

Why, then, does Minsky regard this program, which shows not the slightest sign of understanding, as progress toward the understanding of natural language? Presumably because he, like Bobrow, believes that the underlying 'semantic theory of discourse can be used as a basis for a much more general language processing system.'[5] And why should they think, in the face of the peculiar restrictions necessary to the function of the program, that such a generalization must be possible? Nothing, I think, can justify or even explain their optimism concerning *this* approach. Their general optimism that *some* such computable approach must work, however, can be seen to follow from a fundamental metaphysical assumption concerning the nature of language and of human intelligent behavior, namely, that whatever orderly behavior people engage in can in principle be formalized and processed by digital computers. This leads them to shrug off all current difficulties as due to technological limitations such as the restricted size of the storage capacity of present machine memories.[6] If it were not for such an assumption Bobrow's limited success, heralded by Minsky as the most promising work thus far, would be recognized as a trick which says nothing either for or against the possibility of machine understanding, and the fact that this is the best that an intelligent person like Bobrow could do would lead to discouragement.

2

The formalistic assumption which would lend plausibility to Minsky's optimistic interpretation of Bobrow's meager results is expressed in Minsky's motto: 'There is no reason to suppose machines have any limitations not shared by man.'[7] I think there are good reasons for attributing special limitations to machines, but that is beyond the scope of this paper.[8] Here I wish only to argue that, whatever the intrinsic capabilities of computers, they are limited in their performance by fundamental limitations on the kinds of programs human programmers are able to write for them. Before this can be shown, however, we must be clear what is meant by 'machine', for if a physical organism is to be counted as a machine then man too would be a machine, and the claim that machines have no limitations not shared by man would be vacuous.

A machine as defined by Minsky, who bases his definition on

102

that of Turing, is a 'rule-obeying mechanism'. As Turing puts it: 'The . . . computer is supposed to be following fixed rules . . . It is the duty of the control to see that these instructions are obeyed correctly and in the right order. The control is so constructed that this necessarily happens.'[9] So the machine in question is a very restricted but very fundamental sort of mechanism. It operates on determinate, unambiguous bits of data, according to strict rules which apply univocally to this data. The claim is made that this sort of machine—a Turing machine—which expresses the essence of a digital computer, can in principle do anything that human beings can do, that is, has no in-principle limitations not shared by man.

Minsky considers the antiformalist counterclaim that 'Perhaps there are processes . . . which simply *cannot* be described in any formal language, but which can nevertheless be carried out, e.g. by minds.'[10] Rather than answer this objection directly, he refers to Turing's 'brilliant' article which, he asserts, contains arguments that 'amount . . . to a satisfactory refutation of many such objections.'[11] Turing does, indeed, take up this sort of objection. He states it as follows: 'It is not possible to produce a set of rules purporting to describe what a man should do in every conceivable set of circumstances.'[12] This is presumably Turing's generalization of the Wittgensteinian argument that one cannot make completely explicit the normative rules governing the correct use of a natural language. Turing's 'refutation' is to make a distinction between 'rules of conduct' and 'laws of behavior' and then to assert that 'we cannot so easily convince ourselves of the absence of complete laws of behavior as of complete rules of conduct.'[13] Now as an answer to the Wittgenstein claim this is well taken. Turing is in effect arguing that although we cannot formulate the normative rules for the correct application of a particular predicate, this does not show that we cannot formulate the rules which describe how, *in fact*, a particular individual applies such a predicate. In other words, while Turing is ready to admit that it may in principle be impossible to provide a set of rules determining what a person *should* do in every circumstance, he holds there is no reason to give up the supposition that one could in principle discover a set of rules determining what he *would* do. But why does this supposition seem so self-evident that the burden of proof is on those

103

who call it into question? Why should we have to 'convince ourselves of the absence of complete laws of behavior' rather than of their presence? Here we are face to face again with the formalist assumption. It is important to try to root out what lends this assumption its implied *a priori* plausibility.

To begin with 'laws of behavior' is ambiguous. In one sense human behavior is certainly lawful, if lawful simply means non-arbitrary. But the assumption that the laws in question are the sort that could be embodied in a computer program is a much stronger and more controversial claim, in need of further justification.

At this point the formalist presumably exploits the ambiguity of 'laws of behavior'. Human bodies are part of the physical world, and objects in the physical world have been shown to obey laws which can be expressed in a formalism manipulable on a digital computer. Thus, understood as motion, human behavior is presumably completely lawful in the sense the formalists require. But this in no way supports the formalist assumption as it appears in Minsky and Turing. When Minsky or Turing claims that man is a Turing machine, they cannot mean that a man is a physical system. Otherwise it would be appropriate to say that trees or rocks are Turing machines. These too obey mathematically formulable laws, and their behavior is no doubt capable of simulation to any degree of accuracy on a digital computer. When Minsky and Turing claim that man is a Turing machine, they must mean that man processes data received from the world, such as colors, shapes, sounds, and so on, by means of logical operations that can be reduced to matching, classifying, and Boolean operations. Workers in Artificial Intelligence are claiming that human *information processing* can be described in a digital formalism, while the considerations from physics show only that human motions, and presumably the neurological activity accompanying them, can in principle be described in this form.

All Artificial Intelligence is dedicated to using logical operations to manipulate data, not to solve physical equations. No one has tried, or hopes to try, to use the laws of physics to describe in detail the motion of human bodies. This would probably be physically impossible, for, according to the very laws of physics and information theory which such work would presuppose, such a calculation would seem to require a computer bigger than the universe.[14] Yet workers in the field of AI from Turing to Minsky seem to take refuge in this confusion between physical laws and information processing rules to convince themselves that there is reason to suppose that human behavior can be formalized; that the burden of proof is on those who claim that 'there are processes . . . which simply cannot be described in a formal language but which can nevertheless be carried out by minds.'[15]

Once this ambiguity has been removed, what argument remains that human behavior, at what AI workers have called 'the information processing level', can be described in terms of strict rules? Here the discussion becomes genuinely philosophical, because here AI theorists link up with an assumption characteristic of the Western philosophical tradition, an assumption which, if Heidegger is right, is, in fact, definitive of that tradition. The assumption begins as a moral demand. Socrates asks Euthyphro for what Turing and Minsky would call an 'effective procedure'. Minsky defines effective procedure as 'a set of rules which tell us, from moment to moment, precisely how to behave'.[16] In facing a moral dilemma, Socrates says: 'I want to know what is characteristic of piety which makes all actions pious . . . that I may have it to turn to, and to use as a standard whereby to judge your actions and those of other men.'[17]

Plato generalized this ethical demand for certainty into an epistemological demand. According to Plato all *knowledge* must be stated in explicit definitions which anyone could apply. What could not be stated explicitly in such a definition—all areas of human thought which required skill, intuition, or a sense of tradition—were relegated to mere beliefs.

But Plato was not yet fully a cyberneticist, although according to Wiener he was the first to use the term, for Plato was looking for semantic rather than syntactic criteria. (He was operating on the fourth, rather than the third level of his divided line.) His criteria could be applied by man but not by a machine. And this raises difficulties.

Minsky notes after introducing a common sense notion of effective procedure: 'This attempt at definition is subject to the criticism that the *interpretation* of the rules is left to depend on

105

some person or agent.'[18] Similarly Aristotle claimed that intuition was necessary to apply the Platonic rules:

> Yet it is not easy to find a formula by which we may determine how far and up to what point a man may go wrong before he incurs blame. But this difficulty of definition is inherent in every object of perception; such questions of degree are bound up with the circumstances of the individual case, where our only criterion *is* the perception.[19]

It requires one more move to remove all appeal to intuition and judgment. As Galileo discovered that, by ignoring secondary qualities and teleological considerations, one could find a pure formalism for describing physical motion, so, one might suppose, a Galileo of the mind might eliminate all semantic considerations (appeal to meanings) and introduce purely syntactic (formal) definitions.

The belief that such a final formalization must be possible came to dominate Western thought, both because it corresponded to a basic moral and intellectual demand and because the success of physical science seemed to imply to sixteenth-century philosophers, as it still seems to suggest to Turing and Minsky, that the demand could be satisfied. Hobbes was the first to make explicit this syntactic conception of thought as calculation: 'When a man *reasons*, he does nothing else but conceive a sum total from addition of parcels. For REASON . . . is nothing but reckoning . . .'[20]

It only remained to work out the univocal parcels or bits on which this purely syntactic calculator could operate, and Leibniz, the inventor of the binary system, dedicated himself to working out, unsuccessfully, to be sure, a formal language of unambiguous terms in which all knowledge could be expressed.[21]

Leibniz only had promises, but now it seems the digital computer has realized his dream and thus Plato's demand. The computer operates according to syntactic rules, on uninterpreted, determinate bits of data, so that there is no question of rules for applying rules; no question of interpretation; no appeal to human intuition and judgment. It is thus entirely appropriate that in his UNESCO address Heidegger cites cybernetics (not, as formerly, the atom bomb) as the culmination of philosophy:

Philosophy has come to an end in the present epoch. It has found its place in the scientific view. . . The fundamental characteristic of this scientific determination is that it is cybernetic, i.e., technological.[22]

We have now traced the history of the assumption that thinking is calculating. We have seen that its attraction harks back to the Platonic realization that moral life would be more bearable and knowledge more definitive if it were true. Its plausibility, however, rests only on a confusion between the mechanistic assumptions underlying the success of modern science and a correlative formalistic assumption underlying what would be a science of human behavior if such existed.

There seem to be no arguments *for* the formalistic assumption that all human behavior can be simulated by a Turing machine using syntactic operations without reduction to the laws of physics. (This would be unobjectionable if the assumption were put forward as an hypothesis but, as we have seen, Turing and Minsky treat it rather as a postulate.) Can any arguments be given *against* the plausibility of this assumption?

3

Most striking evidence that such a limit to formalization does indeed exist and poses seemingly insurmountable difficulties can be found in analyzing current attempts to use digital computers to simulate the understanding of a natural language.

Yehoshua Bar-Hillel and Anthony Oettinger, two of the most respected and most informed workers in the field of automatic language translation, have each been led to pessimistic conclusions concerning the possibility of further progress in the field. They have each discovered that the order of the words in a sentence does not provide sufficient information to enable a machine to determine which of several possible parsings is the appropriate one, nor does the context of a word indicate which of several possible readings the author had in mind.

As Oettinger puts it:

[Work] to date has revealed a far higher degree of legitimate *syntactic* ambiguity in English and in Russian than has been anticipated. This, and a related fuzziness of the boundary between the grammatical and the non-grammatical, raises serious questions about the possibility of effective fully automatic manipulation of English or Russian for any purposes of translation or information retrieval.[23]

To understand this difficulty in its purest form we must distinguish between the *generation* of grammatical and meaningful sentences, and the *understanding* of such sentences in actual instances of their use. For the sake of the argument we will grant that linguists will succeed in formulating rules for generating any sentences which native speakers recognize as grammatical and meaningful and excluding all sentences that native speakers reject as ungrammatical or meaningless. The remaining difficulty can then be stated as follows: In an instance of linguistic usage a native speaker is able to interpret univocally a sentence which, according to the rules, could have been generated in several different ways, and thus would have several different grammatical structures, that is, several legitimate meanings. (A famous example is the sentence: 'Time flies like an arrow', which a computer would read as a statement that a certain kind of fly likes to eat arrows, and a command to rush out and clock flies, as well as a statement about the passage of time.)

In narrowing down this legitimate ambiguity the native speaker may be appealing either to specific information about the world, as for example when we recognize that the sentence 'the book is in the pen' means that the book is in a playpen or pigpen, not in a fountain pen, or to a sense of the situation as in the following example from Fodor and Katz:

> An ambiguous sentence such as 'He follows Marx' occurring in a setting in which it is clear that the speaker is remarking about intellectual history cannot bear the reading 'he dogs the footsteps of Groucho.'[24]

The appeal to context, moreover, is more fundamental than the appeal to facts, for the context determines the significance of the facts. Thus in spite of our general knowledge about the relative size of pens and books we might interpret 'The book is in the pen', when uttered in a James Bond movie, as meaning just the opposite of what it means at home or on the farm. When no

specifically odd context is specified, we assume a 'normal'
context and assign to the facts about relative size a 'normal'
significance.

It is such difficulties—specifically those concerning an appeal
to facts—which make Oettinger and Bar-Hillel skeptical about
the possibility of fully automatic high quality machine translation. Bar-Hillel claims that his 'box-pen' argument from which
mine is adapted 'amounts to an almost full-fledged demonstration of the unattainability of fully automatic high quality
translation, not only in the near future but altogether',[25] if only
because there would be no way of sorting through the enormous
(Bar-Hillel says infinite)[26] quantity of information which might
be relevant to determining the meaning of any specific utterance.

Katz and Fodor discuss this sort of difficulty in their article,
'The Structure of a Semantic Theory':

> Since a complete theory of setting selection must represent
> as part of the setting of an utterance any and every feature
> of the world which speakers need in order to determine the
> preferred reading of that utterance, and since, . . . practically
> any item of information about the world is essential to
> some disambiguations, two conclusions follow. First, such
> a theory cannot in principle distinguish between the
> speaker's knowledge of his language and his knowledge of
> the world. . . . Second, since there is no serious possibility
> of systematizing all the knowledge about the world that
> speakers share . . . [such a theory] is not a serious model
> for linguistics.[27]

Katz and Fodor continue, 'none of these considerations is
intended to rule out the possibility that, by placing relatively
strong limitations on the information about the world that a
theory can represent in the characterization of a setting, a
limited theory of selection by sociophysical setting can be constructed. What these considerations do show is that a *complete*
theory of this kind is impossible.'[28]

Thus Bar-Hillel claims we must appeal to specific facts, such
as the size of pens and boxes; Katz and Fodor assume we must
appeal to the sociophysical setting. The difference between these
views seems unimportant to the partisans of each, since both
presumably assume that the setting is itself identified by features

which are facts, and functions like a fact in disambiguation. We shall see, however, that disregarding the difference between fact and situation leads to an equivocation in both Bar-Hillel and Katz as to whether mechanical translation is impractical or impossible.

In Bar-Hillel's 'demonstration' that since disambiguation depends on the use of facts, and the number of facts is 'in a certain very pregnant sense infinite', fully automatic high quality mechanical translation is unattainable, it is unclear what is being claimed. If 'unattainable' means that in terms of present computers, and programs in operation or envisaged, no such massive storage and retrieval of information can be carried out, then the point is well made, and is sufficient to cast serious doubt on claims that mechanical translation has been achieved or can be achieved in the foreseeable future. But if 'unattainable' means theoretically impossible—which the appeal to infinity seems to imply—then Bar-Hillel is claiming too much. A machine would not have to store an infinite number of facts, for from a large number of facts and rules for concatenating them, it could produce further ones indefinitely. True, no machine could sort through such an endless amount of data. At present there exists no machine and no program capable of storing even a very large body of data so as to gain access to the relevant information in manageable time. Still there is work being done on what are called 'associative memories' and ingenious tricks used in programming such as hash coding, which may in the distant future provide the means of storing and accessing vast bodies of information. Then information might be stored in such a way that in any given case only a finite number of relevant facts need be considered.

As long as Katz and Fodor accept the same implicit metaphysical premise as Bar-Hillel, that the world is the totality of facts, and speak of the setting in terms of 'items of information', their argument is as equivocal as Bar-Hillel's. They have no right to pass from the claim that there is 'no serious possibility' of systematizing the knowledge necessary for disambiguation, which seems to be a statement about our technological capabilities, to the claim that a complete theory of selection by sociophysical setting is 'impossible'. If a program for handling all knowledge is ever developed, and in their world there is no theoretical reason why it should not be, it will be such a theory.

Only if one refuses the traditional metaphysical assumption that the world can be analyzed as a set of facts—items of information—can one legitimately move beyond practical impossibility. We have already seen examples which suggest that the situation might be of a radically different order and fulfill a totally different function than any concatenation of facts. In the 'Marx' example, the situation (academic) determines how to disambiguate 'Marx' (Karl) and furthermore tells us which facts are relevant to disambiguate 'follows', as ideological or chronological. (When was the follower born, what are his political views, and so on.) In the book-pen example the size of the book and pen are clearly relevant since we are speaking of physical objects being 'in' other physical objects, but here the situation, be it agricultural, domestic, or conspiratorial, determines the significance of the facts involved. Thus it is our sense of the situation which enables us to select from the potential infinity of facts the immediately relevant ones, and once these relevant facts are found, enables us to interpret them. This suggests that unless we can give the computer a way of recognizing situations it will not be able to disambiguate and thus in principle will be unable to understand utterances in a natural language.

But these considerations alone do not constitute a sufficient argument. The traditional metaphysician, reincarnated in the AI researcher, can grant that facts used in disambiguation are selected and interpreted in terms of the situation, and simply conclude that we need only first pick out and program the features which identify the situation.

But the same two problems which arose in disambiguation and necessitated appeal to the situation arise again on the level of situation recognition. (1) If in disambiguation the number of simple facts is in some sense infinite so that selection criteria must be applied before interpretation can begin, the number of facts that might be relevant to recognizing a situation is infinite too. How is the computer to consider all the features, such as how many people are present, the temperature, the pressure, the day of the week, and so on, any one of which might be a defining feature of some context? (2) Even if the program provides rules for determining relevant facts, these facts would be ambiguous,

111

that is, capable of defining several different situations, until they were interpreted.

Evidently, a broader context will have to be used to determine which of the infinity of features is relevant, and how each is to be understood. But if, in turn, the program must enable the machine to identify the broader context in terms of *its* relevant features—and this is the only way a computer could proceed—the programmer would seem to be faced with an infinite regress of contexts.

Such a regress would certainly be disastrous, but there still seems to be a ray of hope, for a computer programmer could plausibly claim that this regress might terminate in an ultimate context. In fact, there does seem to be such an ultimate context, though, as we shall see, this is equally disastrous to those working toward machine intelligence.

We have seen that in order to identify which facts are relevant for recognizing an academic or a conspiratorial situation, and to interpret these facts, one must appeal to a broader context. Thus it is only in the broader context of social intercourse that we see we must normally take into account what people are wearing and what they are doing, but not how many insects there are in the room or the cloud formations at noon or a minute later. Also only this broader context enables us to determine whether these facts will have their normal significance.

Moreover, even the facts necessary to recognize social intercourse can only be singled out because social intercourse is a sub-case of human activity, which also includes working alone or studying a primitive tribe. And finally, human activity itself is only a sub-class of some even broader situation—call it the human life-world—which would have to include even those situations where no human beings were directly involved. But what facts would be relevant to recognizing this broadest context? Or does it make sense to speak of 'recognizing' the life-world at all? It seems we simply take for granted this broadest context in being people. As Wittgenstein puts it:

> If I have exhausted the justifications I have reached bedrock, and my spade is turned. Then I am inclined to say: 'This is simply what I do.'[29]

or,

What has to be accepted, the given is—someone could say
—*forms of life.*[30]

Well then, why not make explicit the significant features of the
human form of life from within it? Indeed, this has been the
implicit goal of philosophers for two thousand years, and it
should be no surprise that nothing short of a formalization of
the human form of life can ever give us artificial intelligence. But
how are we to proceed? Everything we experience in some way,
immediate or remote, reflects our human concerns. Everything
and nothing is relevant. Everything is significant and insig-
nificant. Without some *particular* interest, without some *particular* inquiry to help us select and interpret, we are back
confronting the infinity of meaningless facts we were trying to
avoid.

It seems that given the artificial intelligence worker's conception of reason as calculation and thus his need to formalize the
ultimate context of human life, his attempt to produce intelligent
behavior leads to an antinomy. On the one hand, we have the
thesis: There must always be a broader context in which to work
out our formalization, otherwise we have no way to distinguish
relevant from irrelevant facts. On the other hand, we have the
antithesis: There must be an ultimate context which we can
make completely explicit, otherwise there will be an infinite
regress of contexts, and we can never begin our formalization.

As Kant noted, the resolution of such an antinomy requires
giving up the assumption that these are the only possible
alternatives. They are, indeed, the only alternatives open to
someone trying to construct *artificial* reason, for a digital computer program must always proceed from the elements to the
whole and thus treat the world as a set of facts. But *human*
reason is able to avoid this antinomy by operating within a
context or horizon which gives to facts their significance but
need not itself be analyzed in terms of facts.

4

In the face of this antinomy, it seems reasonable to claim that, on
the information processing level, as opposed to the level of the
laws of physics, we cannot analyze human behavior in terms of

explicit rules. And since we have seen no argument brought forward by the AI theorists for the formalist assumption that human behavior *must be* simulatable by a digital computer operating with strict rules on determinate bits, we would seem to have good philosophical grounds for rejecting this assumption. If we do abandon this assumption, then the empirical data available to date would take on different significance. The persistent difficulties which have plagued all areas of AI would then need to be reinterpreted as failures, and these failures interpreted as empirical evidence against the formalist's assumption that one can treat the situation or context as if it were an object. In Heideggerian terms this is to say that Western Metaphysics reaches its culmination in technology or Cybernetics and the recent difficulties in AI, rather than reflecting technological limitations, may reveal the limitations of technology.

REFERENCES

[1] M. Minsky, *Computation: Finite and Infinite Machines*, Englewood Cliffs, New Jersey: Prentice-Hall, 1967, p. 2.
[2] *Ibid.*, p. 2.
[3] M. Minsky, 'Artificial Intelligence' in *Scientific American, 215*, 1966, pp. 247–60, 257.
[4] D. G. Bobrow, 'Natural Language Input for a Computer Problem Solving System', Project MAC report MAC-TR-1, p. 102.
[5] *Ibid.*, p. 84. Minsky makes even more surprising claims in his introduction to *Semantic Information Processing*, Cambridge, Massachusetts: M.I.T. Press, 1968, pp. 1–31. There, in discussing Bobrow's program, he acclaims its 'enormous "learning potential" ':

> Consider the colossal effect, upon future performance of Bobrow's STUDENT, of telling it that 'distance equals speed times time'! That one experience enables it to then handle a very large new portion of 'high-school algebra'—all the linear physical position-velocity-time problems. We don't consider it 'learning' perhaps only because it is too intelligent! We become muddled by our associations with the psychologist's image of learning as a slow-improvement-attendant-upon sickeningly-often-repeated experience! Again it is easy to show that what has been acquired by the machine can in no way be called 'understanding'. The machine has indeed been given another equation, but it does not understand it as a *formula*. That is, the program can now plug one distance, one rate, and one time into the equation $d = rt$, but that it does not understand anything is clear from the fact that it cannot use this equation twice in one problem, for it has no way of determining which quantities should be used in which equation. (p. 14)

[6] For example, in his *Scientific American* article (see footnote 3 above), Minsky asks: 'Why are the programs not more intelligent than they are?' and responds

> Until recently resources—in people, time and computer capacity—have been quite limited. A number of the more careful and serious attempts have come closer to their goal . . . others have been limited by core memory capacity; still others encountered programming difficulties. (p. 258)

[7] Minsky, *Computation*, p. vii.
[8] *Cf.* my book, *A Critique of Artificial Reason*, New York: Harper & Row, 1970.
[9] A. M. Turing, 'Computing Machinery and Intelligence' in *Minds and Machines* (ed. A. R. Anderson), Englewood Cliffs, New Jersey: Prentice-Hall, 1964, pp. 4–30, 8.
[10] Minsky, *Computation*, p. 107.
[11] *Loc. cit.*
[12] *Ibid.*, p. 23.
[13] *Loc. cit.*
[14] *Cf.* H. J. Bremermann, 'Optimization through Evolution and Recombination' in *Self-Organizing Systems* (ed. M. C. Yovits), Washington, D.C.: Spartan, 1962, pp. 93–106. In this article Bremermann demonstrates that: 'No data processing system whether artificial or living can process more than (2×10^{47}) bits per second per gram of its mass' (p. 93). Bremermann goes on to draw the following conclusions:

> There are about $\mathrm{pi} \times 10^7$ seconds in a year. The age of the earth is about 10^9–10^{10} years, its mass less than 6×10^{27} grams. Hence even a computer of the size of the earth could not process more than 10^{93} bits during a time equal to the age of the earth. [Not to mention the fact, one might add, that the bigger the computer the more the speed of light would be a factor in slowing down its operations.] . . . Theorem proving and problem solving . . . lead to exponentially growing problem trees. If our conjecture encountered in the field of pattern recognition and theorem proving will not be resolved by sheer speed of data processing by some future super-computers. (p. 94)

[15] Minsky, *Computation*, p. 107.
[16] *Ibid.*, p. 106. Of course, Minsky is thinking of computation not moral action.
[17] Plato, *Euthyphro*, VII (tr. F. J. Church), New York: Library of Liberal Arts, 1948, p. 7.
[18] Minsky, *Computation*, p. 106.
[19] Aristotle, *Nicomachean Ethics* (tr. J. A. K. Thomson, titled *The Ethics of Aristotle*), New York: Penguin, 1953, p. 75.
[20] T. Hobbes, *Leviathan*, New York: Library of Liberal Arts, 1958, p. 45.

[21] This is not the only reason Leibniz deserves to be called the first cyberneticist. His sketchy general descriptions of his 'universal characteristic', coupled with his promise that given enough money and time he could easily work out the details, make him the father of modern grant proposals.

[22] M. Heidegger, 'Das Ende der Philosophie und die Aufgabe des Denkens' in *Zur Sache des Denkens*, Tübingen: Max Niemeyer, 1969, pp. 61–80, 64 (my translation).

[23] A. G. Oettinger, 'The State of the Art of Automatic Language Translation: An Appraisal' in *Beitraege zur Sprachkunde und Information Verarbeitung*, *2*, 1963, pp. 17–29, 18.

[24] J. Katz and J. Fodor, 'The Structure of a Semantic Theory' in *The Structure of Language* (eds J. Katz and J. Fodor), Englewood Cliffs, New Jersey: Prentice-Hall, 1964, pp. 479–518, p. 487.

[25] Y. Bar-Hillel, 'The Present Status of Automatic Translation of Languages' in *Advances in Computers*, *1*, 1960, pp. 90–163, 94.

[26] *Ibid.*, p. 160.

[27] Katz and Fodor, *op. cit.*, p. 489.

[28] *Loc. cit.*

[29] L. Wittgenstein, *Philosophical Investigations* (tr. G. E. M. Anscombe): Oxford University Press, 1953, Part I, § 217.

[30] *Ibid.*, § 226.

7

TACIT KNOWLEDGE AND THE CONCEPT OF MIND*

William T. Scott

Professor Dreyfus links the modern ideal of mind = machine historically to the ancient and authoritative Platonic demand for wholly explicit knowledge. Michael Polanyi's theory of knowledge presents, at long last, a radical and carefully articulated philosophical alternative to that misguided ideal. It is, in its ultimate implications, as comprehensive as the Heideggerian ontology to which Dreyfus refers (indeed, it can be argued, more comprehensive than late Heideggerian ontology, which provokes and suggests but does not construct). Professor Scott has here related this epistemology skillfully and clearly to a familiar landmark in the contemporary philosophy of mind. He may thus lend a helping hand to readers, or, indeed, to the other writers represented here, who, while seeing the limits or antinomies of reductivism, are still groping for the foothold from which they can proceed to scan a new horizon and eventually, in their own good time, to find a new intellectual dwelling place within its bounds.

I wish to show that Gilbert Ryle's account of mental processes as given in *The Concept of Mind*[1] can be significantly extended by considering certain features of the philosophical position that Michael Polanyi has developed around the concept of tacit knowing.[2] The Polanyian themes I wish to employ are outlined in Section 1 and include the integrative and unitary perception of comprehensive entities, the distinction between subsidiary and focal awareness and the consequent 'from-to' relation, the hierarchy of levels in the experienced world, the notion of indwelling and the variability of the boundary between self and world that follows from this notion, and the indefinite nature and function of anticipatory imagination.

* EDITOR'S NOTE: We should like to acknowledge the kind permission of *Philosophical Quarterly* to reprint Professor Scott's paper.

In Sections 2 to 6 I shall apply Polanyian conceptions to a number of problems arising from Ryle's book, including the coherence of the indefinite variety of instances of a particular disposition, the relation between sensing and observation, the relation between mind and observed activities to which mental predicates can be applied, the nature of our ability to recognize a candidate-idea as a solution to a problem, and the confidence with which we can describe mental life in the Rylean manner.

1 TACIT KNOWING AND SOME OF ITS CONSEQUENCES

I shall begin with a brief account of the tacit dimension of knowledge in terms of my own understanding of Polanyi's work. Polanyi uses the term 'tacit knowledge' to refer to the kind of things which cannot be made explicit in speech—things we know and know that we know, but cannot tell. For example, we know how to walk or ride a bicycle but we cannot tell the particulars of coordination and control by which we carry out these muscular activities.[3] A wide variety of examples of this tacit property of 'knowing how' can be given; Ryle himself has several, such as that of the humorist, who knows how to make good jokes but cannot give any recipes for them.[4] Most, if not all, cases of 'knowing how' involve tacit knowledge.

Polanyi shows that tacit elements are also included in 'knowings that' or at least underlie them, in spite of the fact that 'knowing that' is commonly taken to refer only to propositional knowledge that can by definition be articulated. There are, in the first place, propositions held by persons who have not themselves articulated these propositions. The success of philosophers in clarifying thought in a wide range of disciplines is a measure of the great extent of propositional knowledge which is held partially or wholly in tacit form. But there are also non-propositional elements that cannot be fully expressed in much that we know to be the case. An example from Ryle's book is that of an actor knowing the moods of another and being able to act them out, without being able to tell, either at the time or later, what it is that he knows to be the case about the other person.[5] Knowing how to recognize your face entails knowing that a certain face is yours, and yet no rule can be given for this recognition or for any other such case of knowing by acquaintance. Finally, as Ryle himself says, the use of language involves recognizing words on saying and hearing them,[6] a type of recognition that is itself tacit and not propositional.

Polanyi's conception of tacit knowledge goes considerably beyond the mere recognition that there are things we know and cannot tell by providing a structural account of this feature of cognition, which utilizes seeing as a paradigm for knowing, in spite of current philosophical arguments against such use. A basic element of Polanyi's account is the distinction between focal and subsidiary awareness.[7] Focal awareness is the ordinary kind of fully conscious awareness we have in focussing attention on a specifiable object. Subsidiary awareness, in contrast, refers to the peripheral noticing of features of an object that are not attended to in themselves but are seen as pointers or clues to the object of focal attention. Polanyi says that we attend *from* subsidiary particulars *to* an entity under scrutiny, and calls the relations between the particulars and the whole entity the 'from-to relation'.[8]

In terms of J. J. Gibson's recent work, we can describe the focal awareness of a pattern or coherence as the recognition of an invariance in the stimulus information received from the world about us.[9] Gibson also describes the gradients in the stimulus field and the variants occasioned by our moving about, both of which assist us in perceiving the objects and properties of the real world. Such variations in the stimulus field are among the elements that Polanyi classifies as the content of subsidiary awareness. Because the chief character of subsidiary particulars is that we *rely* on them for attending to something other than themselves (that is, the thing we are looking at or listening to), Polanyi is able to extend the notion of subsidiary awareness to include processes of both objective and subjective character, involving all degrees of observability from the fully clear to the completely unconscious. Besides features of an object which we can easily notice, there are subtler clues whose function for us is obscure, such as details of background and context, sensations of colour, pitch, intensity and the like, motions of the eyes, the focussing muscles, and the head that accompany our efforts to perceive, physiological processes that are completely subliminal, and elements of memory and expectation derived from previous experience.

119

While it may seem to be stretching the term 'awareness' rather far to use it for such a variety of more or less subliminal processes, this use has a close parallel in Ryle's extension of the word 'knowing' from the propositional kind of 'knowing that' into the unspecifiable kind of 'knowing how'. To the argument that the term 'awareness' does not properly belong to events of which we are not conscious, the Polanyian reply is that it is neither simple nor straightforward to speak of consciousness of that on which we rely for attending to something else, so that the question of consciousness need not be raised in devising a special term for such occurrences.[10] Once the term has been accepted, we can of course go on to discuss the qualities and properties of the various types of subsidiary awareness, including their degrees of subliminality.

The functional character of reliance by which we attend from subsidiary particulars to the whole not only unites in one category a variety of different processes, but plays a basic role in determining the aspects of things thus sensed in the subsidiary mode. Things look different and sensations feel different when seen or felt as clues to something else, than when they are attended to directly. The kinds of differences that occur depend, of course, on the type of subsidiary element being considered, but in all cases we can say that the knowledge gained by subsidiary awareness is tacit. To speak in the indicative mode about such elements would require focussing attention on them, and then they would no longer be the relied-on subsidiary elements in question. Of course, some of the elements cannot be focussed on at all, in which case only the subsidiary mode of attention is possible. I shall come back to this point below in considering the problem of 'sense-data'.

Polanyi uses the term 'integration' to describe the process of recognizing a coherence from subsidiary particulars. While Gibson describes the perception of information largely in passive terms of immediate recognition, another cognitive psychologist, Ulric Neisser, insists that construction by the perceiver is always involved.[11] The terms 'integration' and 'construction' should not be taken to refer to acts of imposing structure on unformed sense data or of a mechanical or mathematical summation of parts, but rather to mean that the perceiver is active in forming a perception of what it is that he sees or hears, while attending to the object from its particulars. This constructive activity is more evident in cases where perception is not so clear and immediate—'moonlit' in Ryle's phrase[12]— rather than in the immediate, 'sunlit' type of seeing which forms the main burden of Gibson's work.

The integrative activity involved in perceiving coherences is generally rapid and automatic. The mechanism that may account for its operation does not yet seem to have been elucidated, but whatever it is (and whether or not 'mechanism' is the right word for it), we know that we have such an ability. Because of its unobservable and uncontrolled nature, Polanyi refers to it as 'intuition'.[13]

Imagination is a feature which is closely related to perceptive intuition.[14] According to Polanyi, we construct images of what we may see or expect to see. Imagination guides our powers of integration, for instance as we 'home in' on a vague scene in the moonlight. This is not the imagination of a clear, sunlit scene, about which Ryle has a good deal to say,[15] but rather a vague anticipation directing the intuition in trying out various possibilities and providing the basis for judging the successes or failures of the integrative perceptual system in finding out clearly what had been only dimly anticipated.[16] Ryle hints at this kind of anticipatory imagination when he speaks of a person catching sight of a thimble and 'having a visual sensation in a thimble-seeing frame of mind'.[17]

An important philosophical aspect of the from-to character of perception lies in its bearing on the conception of the world as composed of a hierarchical set of levels of complexity and organization. Even without the from-to relation, we know that perceptual wholes are not reducible to their parts, and conceptual wholes are not explainable in terms of laws that apply to their constituents. Ryle has a persuasive account of the latter point in his attack on the 'Bogey of Mechanism' in which he shows that the laws of physics leave quite open the opportunity for an independent set of laws for mental behaviour.[18]

Since for Polanyi, as it was for the Gestaltists, the perceived character of particulars is determined by the whole to which they belong, this whole has an ontological status as a real entity, and not just an explanatory or descriptive status. Ordinary objects, including mechanisms and living organisms, are real things, whose meaning is contained in their organizing principles. What about the principles themselves? I do not wish to enter into the question of whether organizing principles, or patterns, or coherences in general are real existents in some Platonic sense, or are potencies according to Aristotle or to Popper, or have some other status. What is pertinent here is that such entities belong in the same category as propositions, and constitute an extension of this category in terms of representing more complex relations than do propositions, and of being knowable with a more far-reaching component of tacit comprehension. For instance, the concept 'human being' expresses an organizing principle of what it is to be human that defies description and yet is clearly comprehensible not only by human beings but also by a number of species of other animals. Thus while avoiding the question of whether the abstract concept exists, we can assert that the class defined by this tacitly-known concept certainly does exist.

Now if we consider the relation of entities to each other, and the status of parts of entities, we recognize that we can shift attention from a whole to one of its parts, or from a generality to one of its instances, and conversely from a whole to a larger whole, as well as from an organizing principle to a wider one, of which the first is a particular for the second. Each real object or entity of the world is in this respect what Arthur Koestler calls a 'holon', a whole but also part of a larger whole.[19] Since a holon is seen differently when looked at focally and when seen as part of a larger holon, the succession of levels of wholes thus generated, the stratification of the world, has an irreducible character that is a direct consequence of the from-to relation.

Stratification in the world can also be found in the realm of thought. Ryle speaks of many cases of second and higher order processes, such as the increasing levels of sophistication in which we attend to acts of attention. The second-order character of the recognition of the acting out of an action,[20] of the recognition of a person's skill in recognizing the skill of another,[21] and of the imagination of a scene previously perceived,[22] are among the aspects of hierarchical level relations in *The Concept of Mind*. The joint use of several levels is the source of Ryle's concept of a 'thick description'.[23]

At the same time that the world is stratified, it is also unified.

A holon and its set of particular features constitute one entity. While it is true that a part looked at focally is an entity distinct from the whole, subsidiary particulars are only such in being integral with the whole. This point is insisted on by Ryle on the numerous occasions in which he says that an action, for instance, can be described by multiple predicates in a thick description but cannot be treated as being or involving two distinct and independent entities, one physical and one mental.[24] The stratification of the world has no sharp boundaries between its levels.

The relation between stratification and unification could be elucidated by classifying Ryle's multiple predicates into those characterizing an entity as a whole or in some holistic way, and those that refer to a part or a collection of parts of an entity. The nearest that Ryle comes to making this distinction is his reference to main and subordinate clauses in the description of an action, as exemplified by a person pretending to be cross.[25] The person's acting cross may be described by the main clause of a sentence, and his doing it by pretence by the subordinate, or we can reverse the emphasis. While different levels of stratification can be jointly described in this way, the main-subordinate clause distinction fails to show the essential from-to character of our perception of hierarchical relations.

I turn now to indwelling, another fundamental Polanyian conception which will assist in my interpretation of *The Concept of Mind*. The conception is derived from the way we experience our bodies. A person's body is the one thing or collection of things in the universe that the person knows almost exclusively in the subsidiary mode. We rely on our bodies for all our doing and perceiving; our knowledge of our members is almost entirely subsidiary. At the same time, we are aware of our bodies not as identical with our conscious selves but rather as our dwelling places, using the term 'dwelling' to represent that partial and ambivalent way in which our bodies resemble edifices and yet are less rather than greater than ourselves and function more as instruments than as boundaries. Subsidiary particulars occur within us, and yet we live within them.

A fundamental feature of our dwelling within our bodies is that our reliance on them and our trust in them constitute a commitment. We are *there*, and cannot retreat in order to

123

examine our position, for we use our position for all our examination as well as for anything else that we do.[26]

Polanyi uses the term 'indwelling' to describe in the first instance this experienced functional relation of self to body,[27] and extends it by considering particulars *outside* our bodies that we rely on for doing things and getting about. We say that we dwell within a set of particulars, for instance of a tool that we are using, when we are attending from these particulars to something we are doing, or better, relying on the particulars for doing something.[28] In writing with a pen, I focus on the words, the page, and the pen-point, while I am only subsidiarily aware of the pen's contact with my hand and the motions of my hand. These two sorts of particulars merge together in a way that can be expressed by saying that the pen functions as part of my hand, and my bodily habitation is extended to include the pen—I commit myself to it. A similar extension occurs in driving a car, and explains the ease with which we learn (tacitly, of course) where the boundaries of the car are located.

A most important example of the subsidiary-focal dichotomy and the extension of bodily indwelling is that of ordinary speech. We rely on sounds for attending to the words of which they are composed; we are subsidiarily aware of words as we focus attention on a sentence, and in fact as we attend to the meaning of that sentence. We commit ourselves to the conceptions involved in the words and grammar of a language as we come to understand it, and rely on it for thought and communication. In entrusting our mental existence to language, we dwell within it. Language is necessarily public language, so that our dwelling in it makes us inherently social creatures. Ryle's book is basically an account of the language we dwell in and confidently use for describing many kinds of human and therefore mental activity. His very considerable ability to communicate this rich variety of language-use is a measure of joint indwelling in language by his readers and himself.

2 COHERENCE

The relation between a collection of instances of a disposition and their joint meaning can be fruitfully discussed in Polanyian terms. Ryle characterizes a skill or 'knowing how' as a capability

124

for an indefinitely large number of similar actions.[29] How is it that we can identify a skill from given instances of it, and continue to recognize it by perceiving further instances that were not predictable or specifiable in advance? Clearly there is a general coherence among all the actions we lump together as illustrations of a knowing how. We can account for our recognition of a skill if we describe the latter as the focal centre of which the known examples are subsidiary particulars, and around which we can organize new examples as pointers to the same skill. In fact, unless we make some explicit or implicit reference to an organization of particulars into a coherence, we clearly fail to account for our conviction that there is a single skill rather than many or none involved in the actions in question. Ryle gives a hint of this kind of organization when he says of boredom that it is the 'temporary complexion' of the totality of all that the bored person is doing and undergoing.[30]

Similarly, learning something means being able to use concepts and information in a wide and systematic range of applications.[31] We recognize a person's 'knowing that' by attending *to* his knowledge *from* the particulars of his competent use of it. The coherence involved in the concept of knowing how to do something or knowing that something is the case can be generalized to all dispositional terms. If a person has a disposition to act angrily towards an acquaintance, the numerous occasions and types of angry behaviour only cohere into a disposition if we can responsibly integrate these occasions and types into a single comprehensive entity. To characterize a disposition as anger or vanity or any other conditional mental entity need not place it in a wrong 'causal-mechanism' category as Ryle seems to think would be implied,[32] but will place it properly and explicitly in the hierarchy of the organizing principles of mental life.

It is evident that the same analysis applies to the meaning of words or concepts, and also to propositions which relate concepts. The indefinite range of uses of a word or concept, and the indefinite variety of ways in which a proposition can be expressed, point to the meanings of these entities as their controlling coherences. The 'from-to' aspect of meaning shows again that articulate, propositional knowledge is rooted in tacit knowing.

125

Ryle refers many times to the manner in which something is done—intelligently or obediently, for instance—as a characterization in one or another category of the thing done. This is his way of pointing out that we 'read' this or that manner from the particulars. But why stop there? It seems evident to me that we read the presence of knowledge, intelligence, purpose, heedtaking, obedience, or whatever in just the same way.

Mind and body are seen in this light to have a focal-subsidiary relation. More explicitly, the relation of mind to its dispositions is of the same kind as the relation of a disposition to its instances in action. Polanyi describes it by saying that the mind is the meaning of the body.[33] Alternatively one can say that the mind is the coherence perceived when we focus attention on the person, dwelling in the workings of his mind as subsidiary particulars.[34] The mind is 'read' through its overt workings, and in suitable cases can be read quite transparently. Ryle is quite right in rejecting the idea of a completely hidden mind, carrying out a 'second set of shadowy operations'[35] that can only be inferred by some as yet unfathomed procedures from perceptual evidence. In the present view, mind is *perceived* provided we focus attention on it, attending to its workings only subsidiarily. This generality-to-particular relation for mind and body can be called a whole-part relation, since in Polanyi's terms we are relating real entities and not just their organizing principles.

If the workings of the mind were looked at focally, for instance in seeing a person put a piece of a puzzle into place, what is seen could equally well be blind, stupid, mechanical or any of several other kinds of non-intelligent action. Ryle grants that we can see the difference between intelligent and non-intelligent ways of doing things, of course. The only point I wish to make here is that in order to see the difference we must focus on the meaning and manner of doing rather than on the doing itself, and that when we direct our attention this way, the particulars of how a thing is done become seen as pointing to the mental powers manifested in the doing. The *extent* to which a mind is perceived in this way is a separate question, which in the present context might be answered in terms of successive levels of attending from a particular set of mental occurrences to a higher coherence embodying them.

I think it is the combination of just this kind of wholly

appropriate reading of mental attributes from human activity with the wholly inappropriate tradition of Cartesian dualism that accounts for the persistence of the ghost-myth that Ryle attacks so effectively. *The Concept of Mind* begins by asserting that a category mistake underlies this myth, characterizing mind and mental activities as parallel activities to body and bodily occurrences, two cases of the same category with a totally mysterious connection between them. We can now see that this persistent category mistake can be further specified as a hierarchy mistake of the kind that substitutes two collections of parts for a single collection of parts and the comprehensive whole which integrates them.[36] Minds, or more precisely persons, do not constitute counterpart existences to bodies but more comprehensive levels of reality than bodies.

I should like to make one more application of the focal-subsidiary relation before ending this section: a clarification of the problem of whether I can inherently know more about myself than you can. If we distinguish between subsidiary and focal knowledge, we can say that you and I have different sets of subsidiary clues bearing on me, and another range of different sets of clues bearing on you. Each of us can focus attention on me or on you, but the different subsidiary clues available to each of us does not entail that I can perceive coherences about myself that are closed to you.[37] In fact, it leaves open the question as to which kind of observation best provides evidence for which kind of occurrence or trait.

3 SENSATION AND OBSERVATION

Another important application of the from-to relation is to the problem of sensation and observation. It is clear from the discussion in Section 1 that sensations and sense-data fall into the category of subsidiary particulars. We do not observe them focally while observing something in the world, and thus we neither need to locate them nor are we able to discuss and analyse them. Some of the particulars, such as those that constitute our visual field, can be reflected upon and occasionally brought into awareness, but others, such as the physiological items, cannot be sensed at all. Thus there can never be a question of looking at an internal image of the object seen, as Ryle shows from the simple fact that words like 'observe' refer to things and not their sensory images.[38] Both the process of looking and the achievement of seeing can only be described in terms of the external focus of the attention of the perceiver. To attempt a description in some other terms, such as neurological ones, would not only destroy the evidence by changing it, but would also destroy the coherences which define the very processes under study. In the ordinary sense of the word 'data', there are no sense-data.

In my judgment, a better term than 'sense-datum' is 'sensory clue'. Ryle says that having sensations is neither discovering nor using clues.[39] He has no other way to speak of clues than as focally observable, and thus does not consider that clues, whether or not we *could* focus on them, have the character of clues because we *do not* focus on them but rely on them for their bearing on their joint but possibly hidden meaning. For this reason he is forced to reject explicitly the idea that sensations are used as tools[40] for perceptive achievement. In spite of this rejection, however, he effectively grants the subsidiary tool-like functioning of sensations in referring, several pages earlier, to paying heed to sensations without watching them.[41]

Ryle's discussion of ordinary 'sunlit' imagination hinges on the idea that when our imagination brings to mind a familiar picture, it is the act of seeing which differs from that of ordinary perception, whereas the picture may be the same one that has been actually seen. We 'see' a picture; we do not see a 'picture'. In terms of Polanyi's analysis of subsidiaries, we can say that imagination relies only on a set of 'inner' particulars in the nervous system, excluding the retinal and motor sensors that make contact with the invariances in our surroundings. This set of inner particulars is completely beyond the possibility of focal attention, so that it makes even less sense to say that we can look at them than to speak of looking at retinal images.

The language puzzles that develop concerning sensations like itches[42] arise in those few cases where we can actually shift our focus of attention to particular elements of sensitivity. Even then a from-to relation must hold. The knowledge that my finger itches must come *from* unconscious bodily clues, which point from themselves *to* a genuine or spurious source of irritation in my finger.

128

4 TACIT INFERENCE

Ryle tells amusingly how we get into trouble if we try to chronicle the process of making a formal inference.[43] At what time did we first make the passage from premiss to conclusion? Did we repeat the trip, and did we do it hurriedly or did we dawdle? We can present a formal piece of logic in a report or in a lecture to a class, but this is always long after the time we first developed or discovered it. It is the informal process of originally arriving at a piece of deductive logic that can be chronicled, although it is not always easy to do so. The temporal difference between the formal and informal processes of reasoning is reflected in a more fundamental distinction between them, which is that the former are reversible and the latter irreversible. When we present a formal argument didactically, as to a class of students, we hold it up for examination from both ends. The argument can be traced from premisses to conclusion, or followed backward from result to beginning. On the other hand, the making of a discovery, insightful or experimental, is irreversible, for once we have perceived a coherence, its clues change their character by becoming subsidiary to that coherence, and we cannot go back to the state before we perceived the coherence when the meaning of the clues was uncertain and different. Only if a long enough time elapses for us to really forget the discovery can we return to our previous state of ignorance.

The term 'inference' is not used by Ryle, nor by many others, for the informal processes of discovery, largely I believe because of a widespread tradition among philosophers that discovery is a psychological and not a logical process. However, Polanyi's analysis of seeing an object or forming a concept by means of an integration of subsidiary particulars into a coherent focus is a ground for examining the process of discovery in terms that transcend the logic-psychology distinction.[44] His use of the term 'tacit inference' for this method of arriving at truth[45] appears to me to be an appropriate and useful extension of the term 'inference'. It also extends the notion of tacit knowledge in immediate perception to cases in which a set of clues is contemplated for some time before the coherence to which they point is discovered. While the clues after discovery have different aspects

129

than those before, in each case they point to the same thing, once vaguely and uncertainly, and later with clarity.

Tacit inference, thus defined, is seen to belong to the set of mental powers so well described in Ryle's chapter on 'The Intellect';[46] specifically, it is an irreversible one, capable of being chronicled. There are many specialized arts of tacit inference that are developed by schooling and apprenticeship and that take their place along with the more explicit learned skills to which Ryle applies the term 'intellectual'. Among the trained tacit powers are those by which we recognize other intellectual abilities. Tacit inference, like other powers, operates in a succession of levels of sophistication.

One of the characteristics of tacit knowledge is its real or apparent vagueness. Some of this vagueness comes from matters we have not yet put into words, some from unclear, 'moonlit' perception, and still more from the subsidiary character of much of our knowledge. But the widest range of indefiniteness is that which we have discussed above in connection with dispositions. All of the terms used to describe mental events or properties— manners of doing things, varieties of disposition, and so on— have an inescapable degree of indefiniteness in their meaning, for they are capable of application to a wide range of as yet unspecified occasions. Our recognition of a person's skill or of his intelligent learning, as contrasted with learning by rote, rests on a sufficient indeterminacy in the concept recognized that it can be applied to novel and unexpected features of the asserted skill or knowledge.

If the ideal of strict exactness were pursued successfully in a description of mind of Ryle's type, the entire edifice would collapse, for we can only be exact in predicting the results of rote-learning and its analogs, wherein we recognize the *absence* of intellect.[47]

5 ANTICIPATION

A most important aspect of the indeterminacy of tacit knowledge lies in the process of discovery. In Ryle's pamphlet 'On the Thinking of Thoughts',[48] he describes how a person puzzling something out tries many candidates for the statements or arguments or insights that will solve the problem. The person reflects on each of these and decides whether it is an appropriate step or guide for moving towards the solution to the problem All well and good, but what Ryle does not tell us is how a person can make such decisions before the solution has been found. The problem of the *Meno* does not appear to be resolved by Ryle's description.

The answer to Meno that Polanyi gives, and that seems to me to be correct,[49] has been hinted at above in the discussion of tacit inference. We first recognize a problem by a vague integration from a set of clues, an integration that recognizes the clues as pointing to something yet to be found. It is in terms of this vague idea that steps on the way are tested, and their testing involves further steps of intuitive, clarifying integration. The vision that initially was worse than moonlit, fogbound in fact, begins to clear as we move through the fog towards the landscape we are trying to see.

Since the integration of particulars is needed for each trial solution as well as in judgments as to how close the trial is to the correct answer, the continual guidance of the imagination is needed. The imagination is most active in the questing part of the process after starting on a problem and before finally being able to put its solution into formal terms.[50] But even in the statement of a solution, some of the imaginative and intuitive scaffolding[51] erected for purposes of discovery must surely remain, at least for the discoverer, in the tacit integration that allows him to keep track of and to make sense of his formal apparatus.

For the readers or hearers of a formal discovery, tacit components are also needed. The clues by which the reader or hearer constructs a coherent imaginative background that makes sense of the formal presentation come not from the original scaffolding but from a didactic substitute in the form of illustrations and examples, and more importantly although more subtly, from nuances of expression in the presenter's speech or writing.

The innovative and unspecifiable way in which imagination assists the process of discovery is also the way it functions in the much simpler and more common case of ordinary speech. What we are about to say will form the coherence of clues that point to it, primarily clues in the imagination that knows incompletely what it is we mean and are trying to say. To paraphrase Ryle's reference to thimble-seeing, we might say that we begin a certain sentence in an asserting-the-weather-to-be-good frame of mind. Imagination of this sort provides a type of anticipatory mental act that precedes speech and yet does not constitute that explicit private rehearsal which Ryle rejects.[52] It is perfectly consistent with Ryle's monistic view of body and mind to include this function of the imagination along with the more explicit type which he describes, and it satisfies the unhappy feeling one gets in reading *The Concept of Mind* that speech comes, as it were, out of an empty head. Ryle does not mean that it does, but in his effort to attack the Cartesian ghost, he has not given enough attention to our indeterminate, imaginative, anticipatory powers to allow what I think he really means to become clear.

6 INDWELLING

Ryle's disposal of the ghost in the machine is so effective that the value or even the possibility of adding to the argument might well be questioned. Nevertheless, the from-to structure of knowledge does add a new dimension to the attack on the ghost. I described above our dwelling within any set of particulars as a generalization of the way we dwell within our bodies, and the way in which a tool such as a pen becomes a part of our body, in that the contact between self and outside world is transferred to the point of the pen. When we focus our attention on a complex state of affairs, such as writing a paper, we become so involved in the many kinds and levels of subsidiary elements that we come to dwell in them in the same way as for simpler cases of tool-using. I have already described in more general terms our dwelling within the whole range of language that we use.

I see no way of actually drawing the line between such extended indwelling and the purely biological type. I can shift my boundary both outward and inward. If I look at my finger and contemplate the possibility of losing it, I use a narrower concept of myself than usual. The boundary shifts with a shift of the division between the focal and the subsidiary.

Now if the boundary between self and world can shift with the focus of attention, how about the boundary between mind and body? The difficulty in focussing attention on parts of our bodies, and the impossibility of objectifying them in toto, means that the limits of inward shifting of the self-body or mind-body boundary cannot be found. The ghost in the machine was a different object of the same category as the machine; clearly each half of the dichotomy had its own fixed boundary. With the boundary undefinable and moveable, we have another argument against the old dualism.

I pointed out in Section 1 that indwelling is a measure of our commitment. In these terms, we can answer a puzzle that must appear to the more behaviouristically oriented in reading Ryle's book. How can he be so sure and so convincing to us about all his ways of describing mental activity when every term has an indefinite range of meaning and almost none of them can be defined operationally without destroying the whole enterprise? The answer is that Ryle, or any of us, are able to describe mental occurrences with confidence because we dwell in the particulars and in the language used to describe them so thoroughly as to be completely committed to them. It is a measure of our common commitment that Ryle can elucidate from us his readers our confident assent to nearly all of his descriptions.

7 CONCLUSIONS

I have tried to show that the Polanyian distinction between subsidiary and focal awareness enriches Ryle's account of mind by allowing mind to be a comprehensive entity distinct from its overt workings and yet unified with them. The concept of attending from a set of particulars to a focal entity and its generalization in terms of tacit inference, indwelling, and commitment, provide a firm basis for validating Ryle's extensive and illuminating account of mental activities, an account in language of indefinite range of applicability, which requires judgement in application and yet carries with it both clarity and conviction.

While Ryle's account may be taken as part of the groundwork for a Grammar of Scientific Knowledge in the field of psychology,[53] the informal processes of discovery and insight by which we can affirm his account form the groundwork for a Grammar of Scientific Discovery. How we find things out and how we state our knowledge of them in the study of mind, both depend on the from-to relation and on the belief in comprehensive entities that is affirmed by that relation.

REFERENCES

[1] Gilbert Ryle, *The Concept of Mind*, London: Hutchinson, 1949; hereafter referred to as *CM*.

[2] M. Polanyi, *The Tacit Dimension*, New York: Doubleday, 1963.

[3] M. Polanyi, *Personal Knowledge: Towards a Post-Critical Philosophy*, University of Chicago Press and London: Routledge & Kegan Paul, 1958; New York: Harper Torchbooks, 1964, pp. 49–52.

[4] *CM*, p. 30.

[5] *CM*, pp. 262–3.

[6] *CM*, p. 234.

[7] *Personal Knowledge*, pp. 55–7; M. Polanyi, 'The Logic of Tacit Inference', in *Knowing and Being* (ed. M. Grene) London: Routledge & Kegan Paul, 1969, pp. 140–4 (reprinted from *Philosophy*, *41*, 1966, pp. 1–18).

[8] 'The Logic of Tacit Inference', p. 146; M. Polanyi, 'The Creative Imagination' in *Psychological Issues*, VI, No. 2, monograph 22, 1969, discussion, pp. 71–3.

[9] J. J. Gibson, *The Senses Considered as Perceptual Systems*, London: Allen & Unwin, 1968. See also 'The Creative Imagination', p. 56.

[10] 'The Creative Imagination', pp. 56, 72.

[11] U. Neisser, *Cognitive Psychology*, New York: Appleton-Century-Crofts, 1967, especially Chapters 4, 5 and 6.

[12] Ryle quite correctly criticizes the use in epistemology of analogies drawn only from the perception of the 'familiar, expected, and sunlit' type rather than from the 'belated and hesitant recognition, or misrecognition, of what is strange, unexpected or moonlit' (*CM*, p. 303). The former type is a marginal or limiting case of the latter; the effortful species of perception clearly makes a better paradigm for the development of epistemological models than the variety in which the components of effort involved have been lost to view as a result of experience and practice.

[13] M. Polanyi, 'Sense-Giving and Sense-Reading' in *Knowing and Being*, p. 201 (reprinted from *Philosophy*, *42*, 1967, pp. 301–25).

[14] *Cognitive Psychology*, Chapter 6.

[15] *CM*, Chapter VIII.

[16] 'Sense-Giving and Sense-Reading', pp. 199–205; 'The Creative Imagination'.

[17] *CM*, p. 230.

[18] *CM*, pp. 76–82; also G. Ryle, *Dilemmas*, Cambridge University Press, 1954, Chapter V. This point is amplified by Polanyi's recent account of the principle of marginal control, in which the laws of a lower level, say physics, leave open the determination of initial and boundary conditions, which are just those matters that become subject to the laws of a higher level—say chemistry or biology. M. Polanyi, 'Life's Irreducible Structure', *Science*, *160*, 1968, pp. 1308–12; reprinted in *Knowing and Being*, pp. 225–39.

[19] This term is introduced by Arthur Koestler in *The Ghost in the Machine*, London: Hutchinson, 1967, Chapter III, p. 48.

[20] *CM*, p. 191.

[21] *CM*, p. 171.

[22] *CM*, p. 266.

[23] Gilbert Ryle, 'On the Thinking of Thoughts' in *University Lectures*, No. 18, University of Saskatchewan, 1968.

[24] *CM*, p. 50.

[25] *CM*, p. 262.

[26] *Personal Knowledge*, Chapter 10.

[27] 'The Logic of Tacit Inference', pp. 148–9; *Personal Knowledge*, p. 59.

[28] 'Knowing and Being', in *Knowing and Being*, pp. 127–8 (reprinted from *Mind*, 70, N.S., 1961, pp. 458–70); 'Tacit Knowing: Its Bearing on Some Problems of Philosophy' in *Knowing and Being*, p. 160 (reprinted from *Reviews of Modern Physics*, 34, 1962, pp. 601–16); *Personal Knowledge*, pp. 55–9.

[29] *CM*, pp. 44–8.

[30] *CM*, p. 104.

[31] *CM*, p. 312.

[32] *CM*, p. 86.

[33] M. Polanyi, 'The Body-Mind Relation' in *Man and the Science of Man* (eds W. Coulson and C. Rogers), Columbus, Ohio: Charles Merrill, 1969, pp. 85–102.

[34] Ryle's closest equivalent to Polanyi's idea of indwelling is his reference to 'merely thinking what the author is doing along the same lines as those on which the author is thinking what he is doing' (*CM*, p. 55).

[35] *CM*, p. 50.

[36] Ryle implies this hierarchical nature of the mistake in his example of the colleges at Oxford and the University of Oxford, but he does not describe it explicitly in such terms.

[37] Ryle insists that the claim that a person has uniquely privileged access to information about himself is unfounded (*CM*, p. 181).

[38] *CM*, pp. 222–4.

[39] *CM*, p. 232.

[40] *CM*, p. 233.

[41] *CM*, pp. 206–7.

[42] Ryle admits his own puzzlement concerning the language about sensations that arise from such cases (*CM*, pp. 240–4). The approach of this paper eliminates in my opinion most of the difficulties that Ryle is concerned with.

[43] *CM*, p. 299.

[44] M. Polanyi, 'Logic and Psychology' in *American Psychologist*, 23, 1968, pp. 27–42.

[45] *Cf.* 'The Logic of Tacit Inference'.

[46] *CM*, Chapter IX.

[47] Correspondingly, if only exact prediction is allowed for validating a scientific discovery, we are reduced to theories of the type that could almost as easily be artful inventions as descriptions of what is really the

case. It is the experience of unexpected new consequences of a discovery that gives us a true sense that something real has been found.

[48] See footnote 23 above.

[49] *Personal Knowledge*, pp. 120–31; 'The Unaccountable Element in Science' in *Knowing and Being*, p. 117 (reprinted from *Philosophy*, *37*, 1962, pp. 1–14); 'The Creative Imagination', p. 60.

[50] 'Sense-Giving and Sense-Reading', pp. 199–200; 'The Creative Imagination', pp. 64–6. See also 'Genius in Science' in *Encounter*, to be published.

[51] *Cf. CM*, pp. 291–2, for a graphic description of this scaffolding.

[52] *CM*, pp. 295–6.

[53] *CM*, pp. 317–18.

TACIT, SOCIAL AND HOPEFUL

Robert S. Cohen

Polanyi's epistemology was developed in the context of questions of scientific heuristics and its originality is apparent if one compares its approach to such questions with that of orthodox philosophy of science. Professor Cohen, although himself sympathetic in many ways to the concrete, historical approach of Polanyi's philosophy, wishes also to take account of the merits of the more usual 'logical reconstruction' of science.

Concerning the tacit dimension of knowing, which is the first thing and the most important: it appears to me that it is acceptable, and well-established, that there are tacit ways of knowing. This is a most substantial point to emphasize, that this is the case, that one should accept the fact of tacit cues, clues or contexts of discovery. Apparently these are necessary. It is well worthwhile, assuming that they are indeed necessary, to examine the experiment that Michael Polanyi has made—to take this as the center of an outlook upon the theory of knowledge. Right or wrong, successful or not, this experiment is his initial contribution. He didn't discover tacit knowing, but what he did was discover for himself how important the tacit dimension is as the center of an epistemology. Many people—not using that language or those words—would have said the same thing as Polanyi but they have not made so much of it.

1

Taking tacit knowledge as seriously as Michael Polanyi does, we must take seriously all the difficulties that it gives rise to. Here I wish to examine three questions about tacit knowledge.

(1) It appears to me that both in *Personal Knowledge* and in

The Tacit Dimension Polanyi makes an unconvincing and very important reversal, very important to his view, and, if true, very important for all philosophy: namely, that tacit knowing—these semi-conscious clues—depends upon reversed clues. That is to say, the objects we know about are themselves clues to the whole tacit reality of the world. Initially, clues, which we don't know overtly or consciously, are ways of getting at the object, providing situations within which the object is studied. Once we have the Polanyi philosophy of knowledge, we then, as philosophers looking back on knowledge, reach the next insight, for which I find no convincing argument: namely that the fact that knowledge is situated within a background of clues, or a tacit background, means that there is a reality hidden behind the discovered objects. And so objects as we know them become clues to an as yet undiscovered and deeper level of reality. Reality as a whole, then, is in principle only fragmentarily discoverable, but it is more important that in principle reality is marvellously not fully discoverable. There will always be the undiscovered deeper layer of reality, and the way we know about the undiscovered reality at all is by the reversed clue, to use my phrase—reversed in its significance, of course. This suggests that a great deal will hinge on what we do in our philosophizing, in our being scientists, and in our being moralists what to do about the hidden reality?

(2) The hidden reality is one which is given to use by philosophers by what I might call an ontological switch (rather than a reversal of clues). That is to say, not only has Polanyi expanded the epistemological situation from the old and well-justified questioning about how our ideas reflect, mirror, grasp or hold the objects about which they are ideas, but he goes beyond that epistemological question to draw a conclusion from the *fact* of tacit knowing, from its recognition, to a *theory* of knowing, or even to a theory of knowledge, and the attendant ontology. There are ontological levels or layers which correspond to all the levels or layers in the theory of knowledge, he says. 'Knowledge', incidentally, is, for Polanyi, the wrong word; 'knowing', the active word, is its right substitute. Therefore, the 'tacit' isn't satisfactory either; one has to have an action to go with that adjective 'tacit' and the active word is 'indwelling'. Other philosophers have had similar words to serve similar functions—

138

perhaps the word 'participation' to name a way of knowing is another quite synonymous word—but 'indwelling' is Polanyi's proper word for participation in the more overt pragmatic or even the covert Hegelian analysis of knowledge.

But there is one further ontological hypothesis in Polanyi's theory of participation in the tacit, hidden reality, in this indwelling, which I find not yet plausible: namely, that the structure of knowing is quite parallel to the structure of the known reality. We should be careful here. It is not implausible; indeed, I find it somewhat plausible, but it has to be explained why it's plausible. And I must say that I found it not more than a hunch —a very important hunch, but only a hunch, a conjecture—and I'd like more discussion of it. Now this is especially difficult because on this conjecture rests the entire theory of emergent levels: Polanyi uses it *first* for positive construction of what our *universe* is like and, *second*, he uses it as a negative criterion for judging ill of other *theories* of knowledge, including knowledge of life and of consciousness and of cosmic reality. So on this, which is a conjecture without a sufficiently full argument, rests the entire metaphysical strength of Polanyi's position. It's not persuasively argued that, ontologically speaking, there are levels of reality given in Polanyi's philosophy, parallel to levels of science. For he does not relate the two by argument.

(3) The trouble with Polanyi's parallel, it seems to me, is not in its lack of attraction, but in its lack of rational support. As a matter of fact, the same methodological lack appears in his principle of marginal control. The principle of marginal control is Polanyi's scientific way of understanding the relationship among the different levels and the existence of new properties at these different levels of complexity of matter. What for Hegel or Marx or David Bohm would be dialectical relationships of comprehension, or of causality between different levels, becomes for Polanyi a far more scientifically coherent theory, given the name 'marginal control'; but in fact I find that the expression 'marginal control', names a problem, not a solution or an explanation. I have sympathy both with Polanyi and with the targets of his criticism on the issue at hand, at least on behalf of those who want to know in a rational way how it is that matter can think, or how it is that matter can feel. I don't find any more explanatory yield from Polanyi's principle of marginal

control than I do from other theories of the relationship between unthinking matter and thinking matter.

2

Let me examine the force of my reservations by expanding them. Tacit knowing, Polanyi's expansion of the theory of *Gestalt* perception and *Gestalt* theory-making, seems to me to have a fundamentally dark area. I don't understand yet what is offered as an explanation in Polanyi's discussions of tacit knowing. In particular, I wish to see more clearly what is offered as an explanation of differing approaches from epoch to epoch, not to say from culture to culture. It is important for Polanyi to assert that different epochs of science offer different cue maps, different forms of indwelling. Polanyi's way of putting all this is admittedly much more congenial than Kuhn's theory of paradigms or Scheler's view of ideology; but there is something similar in all these theories when they discuss the phenomenon we are attending to: seeing an object in a context which in part is brought to the object. A selection is made from the vast variety of cues; we are told that they, the cues, are filtered out by the ways in which we come to the object and its environment. This is more than a merely physiological fact; filtering is quite often through sociological-historical or philosophical-cultural factors. Only when considering all this may we, perhaps, explain why it is that the knowers, the scientists, of a given time, age, class, sex, race, and whatever else we may have to consider—why the knowers of a certain human type, know as they do, select as they do, *cue themselves as they do*, and so on. Nevertheless, curious as it may sound, Polanyi has neglected to develop this, just as the logical positivists have. Carnap, you may remember, said of the sociology of scientific thinking, that if only Neurath would work this out, we could understand how discovery went on. And Neurath could do it if only he would have spent less time as an organizer. Terribly important as this was, Neurath neglected it; it was so terribly important that Morris coined a name for it. The name was 'pragmatics', but the name didn't help much. Not 'semantics' notice, but 'pragmatics'. Pragmatics presumably would have done—in fact, Polanyi's thesis is a thesis in pragmatics—and I think, in part, it would have been acceptable to the logical empiricists. They would have viewed it as a branch of psychology, but for Polanyi it is philosophy. That doesn't matter much.

Similar to Carnap and Neurath on this matter as Polanyi is, he is also rather different. They specifically offered, partly through Neurath's Marxism and partly through Freudian and other psychological sources, the hope that they would blend the following components into a comparative historical sociology of knowledge. They needed three ingredients; cross-cultural studies, a biologically-based *Gestalt* psychology of knowledge, and a 'pruned' (purified and de-mystified) psycho-analysis. These three components would yield, they had hoped, what would then be an explanation of how it is that a knower comes to objects with a particular set of cue recognition patterns and filters, as well as the raw sensitivity to recognize objectively existing contextual cues. This triple-threat program never was carried out to any extent—there are mere fragments of it. Even these fragments were not carried out by the logical empiricists' Institute for the Unity of Science. There were a few attempts by Philipp Frank, but not much. Some independently-minded Marxists have done something of this sort; the later Husserl did too and there are Husserlian commentaries by the French existentialists.

The Marxists and the phenomenologists alike see in science something, both subjective and objective, much akin to Polanyi's conception. It is subjective in that the whole cue apperception pattern is apparently given, and subjectively given, by a particular bourgeois Western social outlook with its particular pragmatic utilitarian bent. At the same time it turns out, in the course of the three hundred years of science, that nature was, in fact, open to being apprehended in that way. The filter-filtrate analogy holds. And so, to a certain extent, science is objective. All this is shared by these schools; but there is a difference. For all we know, nature can be apprehended in other ways; other sciences, or other contextual apprehensions, other tacit knowing patterns might also succeed within, and work on, the same world of nature. The Marxists allow for that; Husserl and Polanyi seem not to, though for different reasons: Husserl, because of his philosophy of man; Polanyi, because of his ontological-epistemological parallelism. It is hard to say for sure: so much

141

rests on the correct understanding of how tacit knowing takes place that a scientific (or something like a scientific) historical account of different patterns of tacit knowing would be a substantial preliminary task, needed in order to determine how much freedom of variation is allowed in Polanyi's system. I regard this as a major criticism, since I find it not yet attempted, yet significant to our understanding of Polanyi.

3

The same holds regarding tacit powers. This point fits closely with my last point; Polanyi uses a very revealing and profound phrase 'tacit powers' to notice that we convert the impact between our bodies and the things that come our way into a comprehension of their meaning, so that our active role as knowers is a part of the subject-object relationship in given contexts. The very expression, 'we convert the impact of things into a comprehension of their meaning' hides a little obscurity of great import. Is it our comprehension or their meaning? The meaning of what? Do we make *or read* the meaning in or of the things that come our way? Their meaning for us or their meaning in themselves? If it's their meaning *for us*, have we made it into *their* meaning for us? And thereby partly made them? If it's their meaning in themselves, what provides our cues?

Polanyi, with so many others, stresses that knowing is an active process, and knowing makes a difference to the world, or at least it makes a difference to the object or person known, and of course to the knower. But how does tacit knowing give us power to change the world? Answer: by acting on our tacit knowing, not by knowing alone. Here Marx and Polanyi part company since Polanyi says so little about action (although for him knowing is active, which is right). Tacit knowing, says Polanyi, makes a difference to the cues and the context. That is in part where he differs from the *Gestalt* psychologists—and a very important difference it is. But it makes a difference not only to the cues and to the person who does the knowing. A new factor enters here: inventiveness. It is a creative act which makes a difference. Knowing is for Polanyi not only making a difference in some way we're accustomed to; more so it is learning, i.e. it's making a new difference and in a new way.

ROBERT S. COHEN

Knowing is not only mastering the world, and not only changing the world in accordance with some other rational or
ideological pattern; it's far deeper than that. There is a creative
inventiveness, there is almost a divine spark. If there is anything
in Polanyi's epistemology that seems to be close to a religious
component, it is at this point, for it is a matter of cognition that
there is, for Polanyi, that of God in every man. Perhaps even
this idea is already to be found in the Hegelian or the Marxist-
Hegelian way of looking at knowing. But it is unconvincing to
me. First, because the active component linking knowing and
inventiveness in Marx is missing in Polanyi. Second, because it
is a mere hunch or at best a hypothesis that there is that spark
in the knowledge process. Philosophizing this way, Polanyi
attempts to see the cognitive relationship of man and his
environment as a special case of the general relationships of
things to their environment, as a special case of the class of those
interactions, which may be viewed as stimulus-response relations
of whatever kind. Whether amoebas, or higher animals, or
plants or whatever, they all respond in one way or another, and
there is a continuity of these interactions with their environments. For Polanyi, this process is cognitive, though in the case
of man it is one which has made partly explicit what was only
implicit or tacit in others, made overt what was covert in others.
Inventiveness is in the universe, and particularly in man, says
Polanyi.

For my part, I like all this very much. Yet I am uneasy.
Polanyi does not give me a theory about inventiveness—not
even about inventiveness in man. He gives a statement about it,
and I must admit, I find it unconvincing. There is inventiveness,
no doubt. But we want to have a theory of inventiveness as part
of a theory of knowledge. This is a task still to be worked out
rather than an accomplishment. I am so puzzled as to this point
because of the enormous labor and attention that Polanyi puts
on it, yet he has not come up with more than what I have
summarized.

When we set to do a rational reconstruction, we mean to take
liberties. For example, Reichenbach took the liberty of distinguishing between the context of discovery and the context of
justification in research. What Reichenbach says is not that the
actual history of research is to be justified but that the end

143

product of it is justified in that it is given a rationalized 'stream-lined' history, a justification rather than a chronology; a scientist, says Reichenbach, may fumble and be intuitive, etc., in the *initial* stage of his research; but *finally* he justifies it, and so the philosopher's rational reconstruction is not so much a faithful reproduction of stages of discovery as a rational reconstruction of the scientist's own coming-to-terms.

Polanyi, or anyone else, may criticize Reichenbach for his abstraction as abstraction. This is a weak criticism. I think Polanyi has a sharper criticism of this abstraction: it takes an essential part out of the process—its very being a process. It is knowledge, not learning, that Reichenbach reconstructs.

4

What Polanyi has set out to perform seems to be the rational reconstruction of the knowing process. That is to say, Reichenbach sought to provide a rational reconstruction of philosophers' activities; not of scientists' activities, but of the net results of scientists' activities. The logical empiricist wanted a rational reconstruction of a passive precipitate from the knowing process. Notice that if there were a *scientific* theory of the knowing process, the logical empiricists could then have gone on to give a rational reconstruction of that scientific theory. But they were not offering such a theory of the knowing process (nor, *a fortiori*, a philosophical theory). That was to be done by scientists, whether empirical psychologists or theoretical psychologists. The logical empiricists may have been narrow-minded not to want to do that but in any case they didn't. So Polanyi cites Reichenbach on the two contexts, and correctly goes on to protest, that is not a philosophy of knowledge which Reichenbach has given. It loses whatever knowledge is because knowledge is an activity and this is not an account of what knowing is. And Reichenbach, I think, would have agreed. Where there is disagreement is in evaluating any rational reconstruction of the passive precipitate from the activity of knowing. Now, you might ask, what is epistemology? Is it *just* rational reconstruction? The positivists never said it was. Is it a theory of a knowing process? The positivists said, no, it can't be that either, because it also has to include, besides a theory of knowing, a theory of the knowledge precipitated, of the knowledge at the end. Why does it have to be that? Simply because there is another activity to be explicated, other than knowing, namely, the activity of the philosopher of science which is learning and knowing about knowing. To be sure, Polanyi knows this, and reminds us time and again that attention to the knowing process, including its focal and tacit elements, generates a focus on that. Indeed, you philosophers of science also have your tacit, contextual elements, and indeed, Polanyi would want to give a psycho-philosophical account of the logical positivists doing their rational reconstruction. But sophistication aside, it is fair to ask a philosopher, what is the justification for believing in a given theory? What can I know consciously about the evidence for and against, and the probabilities for and against, and the internal cohesion and coherence? It is fair to ask a philosopher of science to tease out what is conventional and what is factual-empirical, what is arbitrary, and what is projected, and what is forced upon us. Conventionalism could be consistent with Polanyi's view about clues and their recognition; but is it? In any case, whatever the theory of conventional, or Kantian, or Polanyian tacit elements may be, it is fair to ask these questions.

The context of discovery and the context of justification, therefore, seem to me not on an equal level. For a theory and philosophy of man, the context of justification is subordinate to the context of discovery, because justification in the analysis of knowledge is after the fact of knowing. Reichenbach is philosophizing at night in the dark, after the day is over, as much as Hegel was and they both said so; Reichenbach à propos of Einstein, Hegel in his *Phenomenology*. But the philosophy of man as discoverer is in the full daylight, and I think Michael Polanyi has the more profound problem to deal with. But how can Polanyi's problem be dealt with unless we confront the theory of scientific knowledge as proposed in the modern tradition of the theory of science? No doubt the history of scientific ideas, as set forth by logical positivist historians, is not a history of men thinking those ideas. It seems plausible, I believe, that the history of ideas cannot be investigated in the logical positivists' way. But the theory of ideas is a different thing from the theory of men having those ideas. Polanyi should not disregard the tasks and achievements of logical reconstruction.

5

If one takes the theme of justification versus discovery, one can just as well make other contrasts which carry the same mental weight. Justification is passive, discovery is active, so the contrast passive/active may generalize this theme. Moreover, we have here the contrast of ideas versus the men who think them. A historical-psychological understanding of science and of scientific knowing would then have to say: all the ideas we have, one way or another, come to us, are grasped by us, and are used by us, with all kinds of associations, not with just the *tacit* knowing that Polanyi singles out, but with all manner of *latent* meanings inherited from earlier usages of those ideas. So that the history of ideas is often simultaneously a history of how a metaphor is purified of its earlier sources, consciously or not, or how a metaphor keeps its earlier meanings but then they become repressed. When they are repressed (I think of such as gravitation, action-at-a-distance, and even attraction, deriving from some pre-scientific source) the original metaphorical content may still have a function, or it may not. I deliberately use the psycho-analytic word because in some crucial cases there is a causal result continuing in the human, functional, history of the idea. In any case, *latency* in the content of ideas suggests one way of looking at this. And the rational reconstructive task would not be as simple as the one Carnap, say, tried to carry out. It would be Carnap plus historical elucidation of the latent, repressed, covert or 'deep' content. It is the entire immediate and contextual, *not just the content of tacit cues*, which matters. Thus, it seems to me, Polanyi's view loses the very historical process of precipitated repression; and thereby also the historical payoff, or at least the historical inheritance that we carry with us.

Take the same argument and use a different intellectual language; perhaps a Marxist, or some other historical materialist analysis of ideology, or perhaps another psychological theory of ideology which affirms that the content of ideas comes from a historical context, which subsequently is imposed on the individual, inherited as it were. The rational reconstructionists would have to uncover those historical, social, or psychological causes and then make clear that the rational content of a given idea is the tip of an iceberg, far more than what was explicit. It may seem unfair to Polanyi to demand all this, but his approach already does so. He calls it forth from the reader, because he not only gives a non-explicit theory of his own, but makes it quite convincing that one must think of such a problem, and seek to explain it. He repudiates a psycho-analytic theory of tacit knowing as insufficient. He repudiates the Marxist (or any other) theory of ideology. It appears to me that much of his own discussion could be re-cast in the language of a theory of ideology and that even the old neo-Hegelian Marxist phrase about 'man as an ensemble of social relations'—if one unpacked the meaning of 'social' and 'relations' (and remember that for Marx, Hegel and Polanyi, man is active all the time)—would suggest that there is a theory alternative to Polanyi's about the very facts he has convinced us of.

Finally, we must address Polanyi's critique of modern philosophy as radically wrong in its theory of knowledge and as claiming something like justification for that strange fusion of skepticism and utopianism to which he calls attention so beautifully.

This seems to me partly right, partly wrong. I don't think he has shown convincingly that the causal explanation of the barbarity of our century lies in an epistemological mistake. To be sure, others have had such a view; notably, F. S. C. Northrop argued that epistemology is the key to a civilization and its fate—politically, morally, religiously. Is this also in Polanyi's writings? But it seems to me that Northrop's thesis is too exaggerated a claim for epistemology; scientifically speaking, much more evidence has to be given to support the view that it has been a mistaken theory of knowledge or a lack of attention to cues or a lack of awareness of covert ideological backgrounds or contexts which turns whole cultures on to disastrous roads. I should say that a lot more evidence would have to be given if that is our fault, because some of the very views which are most closely linked to barbarism are views which, if not fully satisfactory in theoretical terms, are at least successful in their practice. Practices which can manage other people have at time had fully-recognized contextual backgrounds and contextual, even tacit, assumptions, tacit knowings, in the way they have operated. Exploitative theories have, at times been overt, explicit, subtle, discriminating. Moreover, I would have liked to see a closer analysis showing that epistemology in our century has, in fact, had the causal results which Polanyi claims for it—results in general political behavior and outlook.

But that is only part of my reaction. The other part is that Polanyi is quite right; there is a ground for hope. I think his key notion is to understand, from a theory of man which has a scientifically sound recognition of how knowing takes place, that knowing is a successful means of grappling with context; the success comes about from the non-conscious, the other-than-conscious, modes of behavior of man, the knower.

Now, why Polanyi is hopeful is too long a story at this place. But at any rate I see the concept, the dimension of hope, in Polanyi's writings as entirely naturalistic, rooted in the nature of the universe, and by no means assured, a risky hope. Whether this hope—and correctly in great contrast to Heideggerian or Sartrian despair—is justified or not, it is Polanyi's greatest strength. His greatest strength against these continental existentialists is precisely his science, precisely the hopeful fact that the scientist can understand how knowing takes place, can situate knowing as a success of the human animal. This success gives grounds, not assurance, maybe not even high probability, but just simply grounds for hope.

SELECTED BIBLIOGRAPHY*

Ayala, F. J., 'Biology as an Autonomous Science' in *American Scientist, 56,* 1968, pp. 207–21.

Blackburn, R. T., *Interrelations: The Biological and Physical Sciences,* Chicago: Scott, Foresman, 1966.

Bohm, D., 'Some Remarks on the Notion of Order' in *Towards a Theoretical Biology,* II (ed. C. H. Waddington), Edinburgh University Press, 1969, pp. 18–40.

Bruner, J. S. 'On Voluntary Action and Its Hierarchical Structure' in *Beyond Reductionism* (eds A. Koestler and J. R. Smythies), London: Hutchinson, 1969, pp. 161–79.

Bunge, M., 'The Metaphysics, Epistemology and Methodology of Levels' in *Hierarchical Structures* (eds L. L. Whyte and A. G. and D. Wilson), New York: American Elsevier, 1969, pp. 17–28.

Causey, R. L., 'Polanyi on Structure and Reduction' in *Synthese, 20,* 1969, pp. 230–7.

Commoner, B., 'In Defense of Biology' in *Science, 133,* 1961, pp. 1745–8.

Dobzhansky, T., 'On Cartesian and Darwinian Aspects of Biology' in *The Graduate Journal, 8,* 1968, pp. 99–117.

Dreyfus, H., 'Why Computers Must Have Bodies in Order to be Intelligent', *Review of Metaphysics, 21,* 1967, pp. 13–22.

Fodor, J. A., 'Functional Explanations in Psychology' in *Readings in Philosophy of Social Sciences* (ed. M. Brodbeck), New York: Macmillan, 1968, pp. 223–38.

—, *Psychological Explanation,* New York: Random House, 1968.

Frankfurt, H. G. and Poole, B., 'Functional Analysis in Biology' in *British Journal of Philosophy of Science, 17,* 1966–7, pp. 62–72.

Gregory, R. L., 'The Brain as an Engineering Problem' in *Current Problems in Animal Behaviour* (eds W. Thorpe and O. L. Zangwill), Cambridge University Press, 1961, pp. 307–30.

—, 'On How So Little Information Controls So Much Behaviour' in *Towards a Theoretical Biology,* II (ed. C. H. Waddington): Edinburgh University Press, 1969, pp. 236–47.

Grene, M., ed., *The Anatomy of Knowledge,* London: Routledge & Kegan Paul and University of Massachusetts Press, 1969.

* EDITOR'S NOTE: This is not, of course, an exhaustive bibliography. It is intended merely as a guide for the reader who wants to look further into the literature on reducibility. We have not attempted to collect titles on the subject of our last two papers.

149

—, *Approaches to a Philosophical Biology*, New York: Basic Books, 1969.

Hempel, Carl G., 'Reduction: Ontological and Linguistic Facets' in *Philosophy, Science, and Methods: Essays in Honor of Ernest Nagel* (eds S. Morgenbesser, P. Suppes and M. White), New York: St. Martin's Press, 1970.

Hermann, H., 'This is the Cell Biology That Is', University of Connecticut. Institute of Cell Biology. *Bulletin, 10* No. 1, September 1968.

Kemeny, J. G. and Oppenheim, P., 'On Reduction' in *Philosophical Studies, 7*, 1956, pp. 6–19.

Malcolm, N., 'The Conceivability of Mechanism' in *Philosophical Review, 77*, 1968, pp. 45–72.

Monod, J., 'From Molecular Biology to the Ethics of Knowledge', *The Human Context, 1*, 1969, pp. 325–36.

Pantin, C. F. A., *The Relations between the Sciences*, Cambridge University Press, 1968.

Pattee, H., 'Physical Conditions for Primitive Functional Hierarchies' in *Hierarchical Structures* (eds L. L. Whyte and G. A. and D. Wilson), New York: American Elsevier, 1969, pp. 161–77.

Platt, J., 'Commentary—Part I' and 'Organism, Environment and Intelligence as a System' in *Journal of the History of Biology, 2*, 1969, pp. 140–7 and 225–39, respectively.

—, 'Theorems on Boundaries in Hierarchical Systems' in *Hierarchical Structures* (eds L. L. Whyte and G. A. and D. Wilson), New York: American Elsevier, 1969, pp. 201–13.

Polanyi, M., 'Life's Irreducible Structure' in *Science, 160*, 1968, pp. 1308–12.

Prigogine, I., 'Structure, Dissipation and Life' in *Theoretical Physics and Biology* (ed. M. Marois), Amsterdam: North-Holland, 1969, pp. 23–52.

Putnam, H., 'The Mental Life of Some Machines' in *Intentionality, Minds, and Perception* (ed. H. N. Casteñada), Detroit, Michigan: Wayne State University Press, 1967, pp. 177–200.

Rosen, R., 'Hierarchical Organization in Automata Theoretic Models of Biological Systems' in *Hierarchical Structures* (eds L. L. Whyte and G. A. and D. Wilson), New York: American Elsevier, 1969, pp. 179–99.

Schaffner, K. F., 'Chemical Systems and Chemical Evolution: The Philosophy of Molecular Biology' in *American Scientist, 57*, 4, 1969, pp. 410–20.

Simpson, G. G., 'The Crisis in Biology' in *American Scholar, 36*, 1966–7, pp. 363–77.

Sellars, W., 'Philosophy and the Scientific Image of Man', in *Science, Perception and Reality* (ed. W. Sellars), London: Routledge & Kegan Paul, 1963, pp. 1–40.

Smart, J. J. C., 'Can Biology be an Exact Science?' in *Synthese, 2*, 1959, pp. 359–69.

Stent, S., 'That was the Molecular Biology that was', *Science, 160*, 1968, pp. 390–5.

von Bertalanffy, L., 'Chance or Law' in *Beyond Reductionism* (eds A. Koestler and J. R. Smythies), London: Hutchinson, 1969, pp. 56–84.

INDEX

Aristotle, 106, 122
Aristotelian physics, 53, 57
Aristotelianism, 67, 70, 80
Associationism, 25

Bar-Hillel, Y., 107–11
Bergson, H., 2
Berkeley, G., 33
Blumenthal, R., 11
Bobrow, D., 101–2
Bohm, D., 21, 139
Boltzmann, 1, 4
Boyarsky, L., 12
Boyle, R., 38
Boyle–Charles law, 45–6

Carnap, R., 25, 140, 141, 146
Carneiro, L., 12
Changeux, J., 11
Chomsky, N., 18, 83
CNS, 20, 34, 49, 53, 69
Cohen, R., 137
Crick, F., 15–16, 31, 56
C–R Theory, 25

Dalton, J., 28
Darwin, C., 23, 30–1
Democritus, ix
Descartes, R., 23, 34, 66–8, 70, 79
DNA, 18, 27, 31
Dreyfus, H., 14, 99, 100, 117
Driesch, H., 16, 56

EEG, 78
Eigen, M., 1
Einstein, A., 4, 145

Euthyphro, 105

Fodor, J., 108–11
Fraenkel, G., 29
Frank, P., 141
Freud, S., 26

Galileo, 57, 106
General Systems Theory, 34
Gestalt School, 33, 121, 140–2
Gibson, J., 33, 119–21
Gillispie, C., 29
Glansdorff, P., 12 n.
Goffman, E., 96
Gregory, R., 31, 65, 68–73, 75–8,
    81–3
Grene, M., 38, 99, 100
Gunn, D., 29

Harré, R., 15, 22, 23, 25, 26, 28, 29,
    32
Harvey, W., 23, 28
Hegel, G., 139, 143, 145
Heidegger, M., 105, 106, 114, 117,
    148
Hempel, C., 27
Hobbes, T., 25, 106
Hume, D., 27, 97
Husserl, E., 141
Huxley, J., 15

Information Theory, 34

Johannsen, 34

Kant, I., 16, 25, 38, 97, 113, 145

151

Katchalsky, A., 1
Katz, G., 108–11
Keller, E., 12
Kenny, A., 65, 75–80, 84, 99, 100
Koestler, A., 122
Köhler, W., 34
Krebs cycle, 11
Kuhn, 140

Lefever, R., 11, 12 n.
Leibniz, 106
Leucippus, 24
Loeb, 16
Longuet-Higgins, C., 31
Lucretius, 25

MacIntyre, A., 84, 99, 100
Malcolm, N., 46–9
Malebranche, N. de, 59
Malthusian doctrine, 23
Marx, K., 139, 141–3
Marxism, 146, 147
Melden, A., 41
Meno, 131
Michotte, A., 34
Minsky, M., 100–7
Morris, 140

Nagel, E., 16, 25, 29, 45
Natural Selection, 23, 31
Neisser, U., 26, 120
Neurath, O., 140, 141
Newton, I., 19, 23, 24, 29, 38
Nicolis, G., 12n., 120
Northrop, F., 147

Oettinger, A., 107, 109
Oppenheim, P., 16, 25, 27

Paley's watch, 23
Pattee, H., 30
Plato, 105, 106, 117, 122
Poincaré, H., 7
Polanyi, M., 18–19, 31, 117
Popper, K., 122
Post-Galilean physics, 53
Prigogine, I., 1, 14, 99, 100
Protagoras, 17
Putnam, H., ix n., 16, 25, 29, 30

Reichenbach, H., 23, 29, 143–5
Reynolds number, 3
RNA, 27
Rorty, A., 65, 81
Rosen, R., 20, 31, 32
Russell, B., 27
Ryle, G., 41, 117–33

Scheler, 140
Schubert-Soldern, R., 15
Scott, W., 14, 117
Segel, L., 12
Socrates, 17, 105
Spencer, H., 2, 12
Spinozism, 21

Taylor, C., 14, 38, 84, 99, 100
Teilhard de Chardin, P., 15, 29, 61
Theaetetus, 17
Turing, A., 103–7

Weber, M., 26
Whitehead, A., 21
Wittgenstein, L., 65, 103, 112

Ziff, P., 91–2, 94